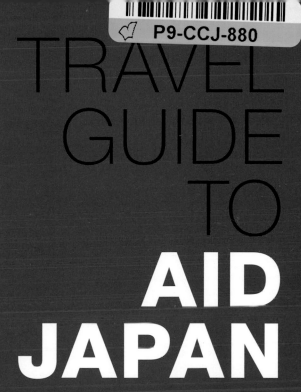

TRAVEL GUIDE TO
AID JAPAN

Editorial directed by **Masanobu Sugatsuke**
Published by **WAttention**

Special thanks to:

Japan Tourism Agency
JNTO (Japan National Tourism Organization)

Akihiko Hirane / Akiko Nakayama / alex-kerr.com /
Ayako Hirano / Brand News K.K / David and Marcia
Cohen / Eko Sato / Emi Hagino / The Foreign Cor-
respondents' Club of Japan (J. Mimura) / Fuyuko
Okui / Gladstone Gallery / HAN Na / Janice Tay /
Jeremy Wilson / Kathleen Massara / Kevin Cooney
/ Koichi Ozaki / Kwihwa Lee / Leemor Chandally /
Matthew Marks Gallery / Michael Mahoney / Misa
Shin Gallery / Motohiko Nakamura / muse pte ltd
/ Rashida Lukmanjee / Research Studios Tokyo /
Seisei Tsukiyama / Takeshi Noda for ZOOLOGY TO-
KYO / Tamasaburo Bando / Toru Hagi / Trysh Wil-
liams / Yoshiki Tsai / Zach Blalock, And All Minook
international(S)staffs

Published by WAttention Co., Ltd.
5-18-10-202 Minami-Aoyama,
Minato-ku, Tokyo, 107-0062
TEL: 03-6418-5701   FAX: 03-6418-5704
www.wattention.com

First printing August, 2011
Printed in Japan

CONTENTS

INTRODUCTION

Since a huge earthquake and tsunami hit Japan on 3.11.2011, the Japanese people have shown a strong will to rebuild the country. The world has also responded with an overwhelming show of support, sending rescue teams and tons of food aid, medicine and other supplies.

But the country still lacks something: tourists. Visitor numbers plummeted after the earthquake, dealing a serious blow to the tourism industry. Without foreign tourists, Japan cannot recover.

Reconstruction is continuing in the parts of the Tohoku region affected by the disaster. Teams are also working to bring the radioactive pollution caused by the tsunami-hit Fukushima Daiichi Nuclear Plant under control.

However, these problems do not extend to the whole of Japan. Most of the country is safe and stable, with the sightseeing spots undamaged and unaffected by radiation.

This tiny book, *TRAVEL GUIDE TO AID JAPAN*,

is a small part of the giant effort to help tourism in Japan recover. The guide features 41 international celebrities who reveal what they like best about Japan. Tour the country with them as they recommend towns, mountains, beaches and hot springs. They also let us in on their favorite places to shop and eat.

In addition, the editorial team has compiled a useful list of the best hotels, restaurants and leisure spots.

TRAVEL GUIDE TO AID JAPAN is a Japan guide for foreigners by foreigners. The guide is not only about traveling for pleasure but also about ways in which traveling can serve as a means to help Japan recover. It is THE guide for those who care and who believe that travel can be a great social contribution. We promise you that, with this guide, a holiday in Japan will offer an extraordinary experience that cannot be achieved from ordinary sightseeing.

Masanobu Sugatsuke
Editorial Director

JAPAN VISIONS

by KISHIN SHINOYAMA

Cherry Blossoms, Mount Fuji

Roppongi Hills, Tokyo

Tamasaburo Bando and kabuki actors at Kabuki-za, Tokyo

A dish of sliced "fugu", globefish

Opinion:
Alex Kerr

Now is the time to
travel to Japan

Profile: **Alex Kerr**

Writer, East Asian researcher and public speaker on Japanese and East Asian cultures. Kerr is well known for his two remarkable books on Japan (Lost Japan and Dogs and Demons). Based on Kyoto and Bangkok, he has been involved in preserving Japan's traditional culture and lifestyles for more than 40 years. Official website: http://www.alex-kerr.com/

Alex Kerr, author and East Asia scholar, first came to Japan at the age of 12 in 1964 and has a deep connection with the country. While majoring in Japanese Studies at Yale University, Kerr traveled all around Japan and visited a small village on the island of Shikoku called Iya. He fell in love with this region, and later purchased a 300-year old thatched farmhouse, which he restored and continues to visit. Kerr has been involved in preserving Japan's vanishing culture and traditional lifestyles there for 40 years. Today he bases himself in Iya, Kyoto, and Bangkok performing consulting, translating, and speaking in addition to researching Asian art. He has the reputation of being a person with an especially high level of understanding of Japanese tradition and culture.

On March 11, when the 8.9 magnitude earthquake hit Japan, Kerr was waiting for his flight to Thailand at Narita Airport. He was surprised at the aftershocks of a strength that he had never before experienced. He was stunned further by the devastating tsunami footage on internet news sites. Five days later he returned to Japan and found very few foreigners in the airport. Now he encourages that people "visit Japan to save Japan." Here is his message:

After the quake I came back to Kansai (the southern-central region of Japan) on March 16 because my business activities are based here. After the massive earthquake, the response of the Japanese people – their politeness and maintenance of order at a time of disaster – were praised worldwide. In Kansai, however, daily life did not change. People there weren't particularly polite or impolite. It could be said that western Japan, hundreds of kilometers away from seriously earthquake-affected areas, received almost no impact. Regardless, Kansai has lost a number of tourists. My business is mainly related to inbound tourism and many of my partners have been suffering as a result of this drop.

Harmful rumors Japanese products and Japan itself have long enjoyed a well-earned reputation internationally for safety and efficiency. However, the crisis at the Fukushima Daiichi nuclear plant resulted in a loss of reputation and, unfortunately, some incorrect information about the effects of radiation spread around the world. I went to Thailand again in April and read news reports of their authorities having an emergency meeting regarding Japanese food imports; however, as far as I know, most of Thailand's people are not being misled by harmful rumors.

Unfortunately, it is a fact that certain imported Japanese goods may possibly be contaminated by nuclear radiation. Japan's management of the situation is being watched closely by other countries that may take protective measures against radiation. I think the harmful rumors will gradually disappear once the Japanese government takes control and provides full disclosure.

Fly to Japan The disaster has resulted in a sharp decrease in the number of international tourists to Japan. I would say it is a kind of panic. The evacuated area around the Fukushima Daiichi nuclear plant is dangerous, of course. However, the Kansai and Kyushu regions, hundreds of kilometers away from the plant, are totally safe. You don't need to worry about Tokyo, either.

Meanwhile, Japanese people value the concept of *jishuku* ("self-restraint" in order to show sympathy for the sorrow of others), and this caused a big decline in Japanese tourism all around the country. However, for the sake of rebuilding the country quickly, economic activity should be promoted as it was before. I encourage people to travel within Japan and promote Japanese events. Proceeds from these events can be used to help the Tohoku region.

One trip I could recommend is around western Japan. I've had a strong relationship with Shikoku for years, especially the mountain village of Iya, in Tokushima Prefecture, where I have my house Chiiori. (The name

Chiiori, an old thatched farmhouse built in Iya Valley. It shares the dream of building an eco-friendly community with the volunteer community based around the house. For more information, visit http://www.chiiori.org/en/index.html

"Chiiori" means "The House of the Flute"). It's an old thatched farmhouse that was built in the 18th century. Iya Valley preserved a number of traditional thatched-roof *minka* houses up until a few decades ago. Chiiori, and the volunteer community based around it, shares a dream with many people; the dream of building an eco-friendly community that is deeply rooted in Japan's traditional culture. You can stay at this place with an advance reservation.

There are many more attractions in Shikoku. Along the coast there are breathtaking views of the Seto Inland Sea. You can enjoy a cruise out on the water to watch a stunning sunset with small islands forming a gorgeous background for the scene. I, myself, love the rainy season from early June to early July because the fog-shrouded mountains look mysteriously beautiful in the mists.

For art connoisseurs, Shikoku is a must-visit destination. The Isamu Noguchi Garden Museum in Takamatsu, Kagawa prefecture exhibits over 150 artworks from prominent Japanese-American modern sculptor Isamu Noguchi (who died in 1988). The museum preserves the working atmosphere of his studio. Naoshima, a small island, is known for its picturesque views and unique art galleries. The fascinating exhibits include The Benesse Art Site Naoshima, which provides visitors with the experience of a museum inside a hotel. In the old town, The Art House Project showcases outstanding installations that combine the island's traditional architecture with contemporary art.

Moreover, the region is best known for the Shikoku Pilgrimage. This is the practice of visiting the 88 temples of the pilgrimage associated with the 9th century Buddhist monk Kukai. It is said that wishes come true after completion of the pilgrimage. Also worth visiting is a shrine called "Konpira-san," located on a steep mountainside. It has been used for worship since the Edo period.

Visiting popular spots or taking tours are both good ideas, but I also recommend you try to make your own unique, adventurous trip.

Rebuilding Japan   What can we do now for Japan after suffering the Great Eastern-Japan Earthquake? Donating money is one easy and quick way, though really the best thing people can do is to simply go about their daily business. If you already had plans to fly to Japan, then please do so. Once the various regions of Japan return to normalcy, Tohoku will recover too. If you were interested in Japan before the disaster, don't consider Japan to now be unsafe. Your decision will help lead Japan's revitalization. Now is the time to travel to Japan.

Even in the northeast, while the earthquake and tsunami left serious damage along the coastal areas of Tohoku, inland there is no destruction.

Inside of Chilori

In January 2011, I visited Tohno City, in Iwate Prefecture, a place known as the land of old folk tales. Tohno is a picturesque area where you can find L-shaped farmhouses called "Magariya." Kappabuchi Pool, where it is believed the Kappa (an elfish creature with a dish-shaped head) lived, is also very charming.

This area remains just as beautiful as it was in the past. It is not true that all of Tohoku or most other parts of Japan face danger, since radiation exposure concerns are primarily serious only in the Fukushima area.

Rebuilding of the earthquake-affected areas has just begun. Some of the tsunami-impacted areas were already suffering from depopulation, much like other rural areas in Japan. I would suggest that we must create innovative plans rather than focusing on simply pumping cash into public works. If there are any movements to reconstruct affected areas, I would absolutely like to help.

HOW TO ENJOY THIS GUIDE

Celebrities' Recommendations

In this guide you will find celebrity recommendations about Japan. Their comments are listed alphabetically by first name. In an effort to give you the celebrities' words directly, we haven't changed the way they write. You'll find their profile, photo, length of stay and number of visits to Japan at top of each page. You will get original ideas to make your trip memorable and fun.

Editor's Memos

The more you read this guide, the more you may want to know about recommended sites and activities. Editors chose some recommendations to explain in greater detail.

Maps, photos and captions

Photos are always easy and useful ways to get ideas about things you want to know. We've included a number of photos showing places and scenes that Japan is proud of, as well as informative captions. Also, we note locations on a small map above the photos.

DESTINATION DIRECTORY Recommended by editors

Can't choose your destination? No problem. We have an index of accommodation facilities, onsen (hot springs), restaurants, museums, World Heritage Sites, shrines, and temples. Moreover, there is information for those interested in volunteering to help earthquake affected areas.

TRAVEL GUIDE TO AID JAPAN

41 celebrities and
cultural figures worldwide
aid Japan with tourism

Allan West , U.S.A.

recommends:
Ueno/Yanaka area of Tokyo

Artist--working in the Yamato-e tradition. He express-
es the abundant glory of the natural world on folding
screens and hanging scrolls.

Length of stay: 30 years

I recommend the Ueno/ Yanaka area to my friends visiting Tokyo. You can stay at Sawanoya, or Katsutaro, traditional Japanese inns right in the center of Yanaka, Tokyo's historical neighborhood. The National Museum complex in nearby Ueno Park began as the Imperial art collection. The restaurant there at the Horyuji annex is excellent. Ueno Park hosts month-long flea markets each season to coincide with the cherry blossoms, the lotus in bloom, the autumn leaves, and New Years festivities at the island temple of Benten. The park was a popular attraction for citizens from the 17th century as it was set up to resemble a map of Japan in miniature.

Representations of Kyoto's Kiyomizu-dera Temple, Nikko's Toshogu, the Benten shrine in Lake Biwa are some of what remains of this curious history. Starting from 1877, the park has hosted over seven Expos - the effect we see today in the museum and zoo that originated as part of the events.

While in the park, visit the Shitamachi Museum, for a taste of 19th and early 20th century Tokyo. From there, just walking around the Yanaka temple district is a pleasant way to enjoy the quiet side of Tokyo. With the greatest number of temples for the area in all of Japan, you can enjoy gardens, temple architecture, and the smell of incense on your way. Yanaka began as a spiritual center over 400 years ago as a way to protect the city of Edo (as Tokyo before the 19th century was called) from evil influences.

A little further, and you can see Yanaka Ginza, one of Japan's most vibrant outdoor neighborhood shopping streets. The Ueno/ Yanaka area is also famous for its artists. Artists who served both the Shogun, and the temple complex lived in Yanaka. Later, with the expositions, and the establishment of the Tokyo University of the Arts in 1876, more artists congregated. In this area, you can enjoy the arts with 14 museums and three concert halls in Ueno, and over 20 galleries in Yanaka. The homes and studios of famous artists such as the painter Yokoyama Taikan and sculptor Asakura Fumio (restoration work to be completed in the Spring of 2013) are also open for a visit. You may even get a glimpse of me at work in my Yanaka studio.

With a 250 year-old temple's facade, West's studio gallery in Yanaka's temple district blends in well with its surroundings.

Andreas Gursky, Germany

recommends:

Japanese cathedral of science

Visual artist best known for his large-scale, colour photographs that explore and reflect the effect of capitalism and globalisation on contemporary life.

Number of visits: 4 times.

To realize the art work "Kamiokande," in 2007, I visited the neutrino-lab in a former mine not far from the Japanese community of Kamioka in Gifu Prefecture. The neutrino-tank pictured is for the study of elementary cosmic particles and normally filled with water. Due to an internal overhaul, the tank was temporarily emptied. This procedure allowed me to capture this exceptional view into this Japanese cathedral of science.

Editor's memo KamiokaNDE: detecting neutrios under ancient mines

---

KamiokaNDE (Kamioka Nucleon Decay Experiment) is a neutrino physics laboratory located 1,000 meters underground under the former mines in Kamioka, a section of Hida City in Gifu Prefecture. It was built here in 1983 due to its firm geological property, abundant source of water and stable temperature. In 1987, a group led by Dr. Masatoshi Koshiba detected neutrinos for the first time in the world, and Dr. Koshiba was jointly awarded the Nobel Prize in Physics in 2002. The facility was shut down in 1996 when the new and improved Super Kamiokande started up close by.

Kamioka is a town surrounded by mountains in northern part of Gifu. Mining in the town dates back to early 8th century and, until its closure in 2001, produced a large amount of zinc, lead and silver. The town also has Wariishi Onsen a public hot spring, and Kamioka Castle, originally built in1564, destroyed in 1615 and partly rebuilt in 1970.

Kamioka

Gifu

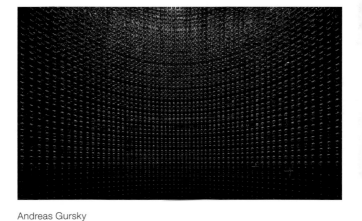

Andreas Gursky
Kamiokande, 2007
C-Print
357 x 222 x 6,2 cm
Copyright: Andreas Gursky / VG Bild-Kunst, Bonn 2011 Courtesy Sprüth
Magers Berlin London

Andrew W.K. , U.S.A.

recommends:
Pachinko

Multi-faceted musician and performer. He calls himself "a professional partier, a rock 'n' roll singer, a TV person, an entertainer."

Number of visits: almost 20 times

I absolutely love the game Pachinko. It's hard to miss the powerful presence of the Pachinko parlors, all around the cities. They're loud, bright, colorful, and full of Pachinko machines! Pachinko is one of my favorite things in the whole wide world. It's like a combination of pinball, slot-machines, and something very unique to Japan. As a player, you launch small silver balls into a vertical play-field covered with small nails which cause the balls to bounce around. If the balls bounce into the right areas, you can win even more balls! Then you can trade in the balls you won in for prizes and special gifts! I love it so much – the atmosphere of the parlor is really amazing!

When I first visited Japan as a 13-year-old, my brother and I would explore all around the streets of Kyoto, where we were staying in a rented apartment. It was cool how the streets were so safe, that my Mom could let us go around by ourselves without any worries. We would go into the Pachinko parlors and pick up loose balls from the floor and try to play with them.

Everyone was really nice! Many years later, after I started coming to Japan to perform and do my entertainment work, I had the chance to play Pachinko much more often, and legally! The first time I really sat down to play for an extended period of time, I actually got a "FEVER" (like a jackpot) and won thousands of balls. I traded them in and was a real winner! It was honestly one of the happiest days of my life.

I'm not sure if we were legally old enough to be playing.

Pachinko

Inside of a pachinko parlor in Japan. Pachinko is a gaming device that is similar in concept to the slot machine and pinball.

Catarina Hong, Brazil

recommends:

Things in Tokyo

Reporter at Record TV - Brazil, one of the largest broadcasting network in Brazil. Asia correspondent for a bit more than 4 years.

Length of stay: from Jan 2006 to May 2010

TSUKIJI FISH MARKET - Anyone who goes to Tokyo has to take advantage of the jet lag – especially if you're coming from North, Central or South America. Why not go to a fish market at 5am? For me, the number one must-see place in Tokyo is the Tsukiji Fish Market – which is bubbling in the early morning hours. It's been written about a thousand of times and there is no guide book about Tokyo that doesn't mention it. The variety of sealife is stunning. I've seen the weirdest, most exotic fish there, and of course, the tuna auction. Actually more interesting than the auction itself, and the incredible amount of tuna sold are the mannerisms and personalities of the auctioneers. Don't leave without tasting the freshest sushi of your life. And if you want another reason to wake up early for the fish fest at Tsukiji, the local government has been threatening for years to relocate the market.

SHIMOKITAZAWA - Harajuku is interesting and fun but there's a less touristy and more artistic crowd outside of the Yamanote Line. In Shimokitazawa, you can dig for treasures in small shops, cafés and used record shops. At night, you can find anything from hardcore to folk and hip hop in any of the dozens of local live music venues.

SAVOY PIZZA - After you've stuffed yourself with *kaiten-sushi* and street *yakisoba*, you should definitely have some pizza. It's not any pizza. It's THE pizza. I could've never imagined that I'd have the best pizza of my life in Tokyo. Savoy is a hole-in-the-wall pizzeria where the wood oven and the counter takes up most of the space. They use the best ingredients of Japan and Italy to produce only two types of pizzas: napolitana and marinara. Order both with some spicy ginger ale. And if you get acquainted to the pizzaiolo – which is very easy, they're all really cool – he might treat you with some inventive granita.

Shimokitazawa
Tokyo

Shimokitazawa is a town that is popular among the young for its many second hand clothing shops and variety stores.

David Bintley, U.K.

recommends:

Tokyo

Artistic Director of The National Ballet of Japan, at The New National Theatre Tokyo. Also Director of The Birmingham Royal Ballet in England.

Length of stay: approximately 4 months per year

Although I am a great admirer of Japan and its culture my work keeps me pretty well confined to Tokyo and it's environs. However, the City is an extraordinary metropolis with so many great places to eat and drink and so many wonderful historic sites to see that after frequent visits over the past five years, I don't feel I've even scratched the surface.

If you like 'Western' Art however, and Opera and Ballet have a huge following in Japan, then The New National Theatre is a must. The theatre is only fourteen years old and must be one of the greatest opera houses in the world with three beautiful stages that regularly present the world's greatest operas and ballets as well as cutting-edge contemporary dance and award-winning drama. The theatre is only one metro stop away from the exhilarating Shinjuku area, with it's exciting night-life.

If your curiosity makes you want to seek out more traditional Japanese arts however, then the National Theatre (not 'New'!) is where you should head. I have been a fan of Kabuki for many years but I recently saw my first Bunraku performance at the National and I was absolutely knocked out. If you've never seen this wonderful mixture of music, story-telling and puppetry then get along to this great theatre and let these masterly performers astonish you.

A scene of "Kotobuki-Shiki-Sanbaso" of Bunraku from the National Theatre's 45th anniversary play. Bunraku is the traditional Japanese puppet theatre, in which puppets are skillfully manipulated to act out a narrative recited to the accompaniment of the shamisen. Photo provided from National Theatre

Denis Lavant, France

recommends:

Tokyo in early winter

Actor known for his distinctive face and the physically demanding aspects of the roles he plays. Often appears on director Leos Carax's films.

Number of visits: 1 time

I visited Japan for the filming of "Tokyo!," an anthology film. I appeared in one of three segments directed by Leos Carax. It was in December but not too cold for me. It was rather comfortable. I spent times only in the winter, so that I would recommend visiting Tokyo in early December.

If you travel in Japan, I want you to enjoy not only big cities like Tokyo, but also countryside. Walking around by yourself in Tokyo is hard to miss. I simply like walking to find interesting towns. Urban taste of Tokyo also attracts me. I can easily find buildings, shops, and crowds. If I walk some more blocks, there will be a quiet place with a number of two-story houses. Tokyo is where you will see both modernity and quietness.

I stayed in Shibuya and I saw white swans on a pond where was only 500 meters away from the hotel. It was like my home town located in the suburbs of Paris. When I felt hungry, I often went to a sushi bar that can be easily found. I savored sushi and green tea standing up. I love the convenience of Tokyo.

On weekends, please visit onsen towns located two hours away from Tokyo. Enjoy a hot spring with the view of beautiful sea. I was very happy as if I were a frog. Then I hiked in the hills by myself and found magnificence of nature. I would say the nature in Japan is gentle and calm. It is also romantic that you will see Akira Kurosawa's movies.

Just steps from the neon frenzy of Shibuya, Nonbei Yokocho is a retro alley of tiny bars lined with willow trees and lanterns. The proximity of mega-city and village makes Tokyo uniquely enjoyable.

Derek Lam, U.S.A.

recommends:

Dining, the view of Tokyo

Fashion designer. Established Derek Lam Company together with Jan-Hendrik Schlottmann in 2002. Launched his first collection in Spring 2004.

Number of visits: more than 10 times

D ining is one of my favorite things to do in Japan. Everything there is great, so I always enjoy looking around on the basement floor in department stores. I visited the Tsukiji Fish Market five years ago. It was very early in the morning but I could see Japanese unique culture there.

I like the mid-century interior design and hospitality in Hotel Okura. The building is magnificent. The staff and hospitality are highly professional.

The view of Tokyo is my favorite scenery. I like to have dinner at the New York Grill on 52nd floor in the PARK HYATT TOKYO. The atmosphere connects New York and Tokyo. I feel comfortable there. I can also feel Japanese traditions as well.

Editor's memo   Tsukiji: widely known for its large fish market

Tsukiji is located along the Sumida-gawa River, lying next to Tokyo's exquisite town Ginza. The area is best known for its fish market, which is also called "*Uogashi* (fish market)." The Tsukiji Market handles the largest volume of fishery products in Japan, with more than 450 kinds of products, such as tuna, dealt around-the-clock, this market is unique throughout the world. The well-known "*Seri*" auctions begin at 5:00 AM and ends by 8:00 AM. The market is crowded with people buying fresh products from the specialized dealers or having breakfast there.

Dick Lee, Singapore

recommends:

History, culture, food and nature

Singaporean pop singer, composer, songwriter, and playwright. He is often referred to as a spokesperson for New Asian generation.

Number of visits: many times since he was a teenager

Japan is a very beautiful country, in spite of the earthquake, most of the country's beauty remains intact. There is so much to enjoy: Japan's deep history and culture, amazing food, majestic nature, and everything that's new and forward-looking in the country. Personally, I enjoy Tokyo, its dynamic energy and astonishing and endless shopping choices. Everything is of such high quality and presented so elegantly with the highest standard of service in the world.

Editor's memo   A treasure island: Delicious delicious delicious!

Sushi, tempura and teriyaki have become a global sensation, but there are many more extraordinary dishes in Japan. Japanese people value seasonality and regionality in their dishes that one dish, cheap or expensive, could have a great variety throughout the year and in different regions. In traditional full course meal, *kaiseki*, the picturesque presentation of the food, not to mention its deliciousness, takes the experience of eating to another level. There is also a variety of popular "everyday" dishes offered at reasonable price. Different types of noodles such as ramen, *udon* and *soba* as well as *donburi* (meat or fish served on rice) are delicious and usually under 1,000 yen.

Also, try fresh tofu. It will blow your mind!

Don't be shy, and try as many dishes as possible!

Eric Khoo, Singapore

recommends:

Manga culture

Film director/producer. His first feature Mee Pok Man was invited to renowned film festivals and won prizes at Fukuoka, Pusan and Singapore.

Number of visits: 5 times, about 1 week each time

Mandarake shops (a comics and toy collectible store), the Nakano Broadway Mall, Akihabara and Shibuya. The Tezuka Museum in Osaka.

I have always had a fascination about Japanese culture, especially, its deep ingrained influence in the area of comics and toys. During the past year while spending time in Tokyo working on my new animation film, Tatsumi, I had the opportunity to spend more time in places like Mandarake and Akihabara. They are indeed the mecca for lovers of comics and toy collectors like me.

Last year, I also made a trip to Osaka where Mr. Yoshihiro Tatsumi grew up. I visited the Tezuka Museum and there I saw many characters that were created by Mr. Osamu Tezuka. They brought back many fond memories as I used to watch many of these characters on TV as a kid.

Editor's memo   Manga culture is now heart of pop culture

Manga is a Japanese popular culture, and is widely read among almost all age groups. Today manga and animation culture has spread through the world. There are a number of manga related facilities such as manga *kissa*, a cafe where people spend time reading manga, surfing the internet, and even taking naps.

Nakano Broadway, is a shopping center located right in front of Nakano train station north exit. On the 2nd to 4th levels of Nakano Broadway, more than half of the shops are for peoples who like Japanese subcultures.

Ferran Adrià, Spain

recommends:

Tokyo and Kyoto

Head chef of the El Bulli restaurant in Roses on the Costa Brava. Loves his profession and admire Japan and its culture.

Number of visits: 5 times

Y ou should have an extensive vist in the city of Tokyo. The whole city is always full of surprises. As a cook and also personally, I like Tsukiji Fish Market. Traditional shops, sushi and soba restaurents around the market and Kappabashi area in Asakusa are also wonderful. I also recommend visiting Japanese department stores where every single product is so delicately displayed, which is so impressive to us foreigners.

But, in general, any place is nice. Kyoto, for example, is one of the most mesmerising cities I have ever visited.

This is because you can discover the culture that is unimaginable, in terms of people's politeness and the attention they pay to things, and their culture is completely different from ours. As soon as you take your first step there, you will certainly feel that everyone is kind and that you came to a place where people welcome you with at most care and generousity. Japanese hospitality is extraordinary.

Editor's memo　Asakusa: Feel old atmosphere of Tokyo

Asakusa used to be Tokyo's leading entertainment district since the Edo Period with kabuki theaters, and near by Yoshiwara, the largest and famous red light district until 1958. In the Meiji and Taisho Peiods, modern types of entertainment facilities such as movie theaters were established in the district.

Kappabashi, sometimes known as "kitchen town" is an 800-meter-long street that stretches from the intersection at Kikuya bridge down to Kototoi-dori Street. This area specializes in supplying crockery, furniture, ovens and decorative items to the restaurant trade in Tokyo.

Florence Deygas, France

recommends:

Hakone

Visual artist, makes drawings, and together with Olivier Kuntzel, under the name Kuntzel+Deygas, creates narrative design and videos.

Number of visits: more than 10 times since 1994

For Tokyo visitors, it is easy to jump for a few days to this delicate and relaxing place that seems so out of the scope of time: Just take the "Romancecar" to Hakone, then take this old-fashioned train up to the mountains. Climb over flowers and get from the forest with its extraordinary and subtle smell to the village called Gora. The Kansuiro Ryokan is 400 years old and fortunately it has kept its authenticity, both the good and bad sides! It's NOT comparable at all to the usual contemporary international standards of luxury and comfort, and that's exactly what I love about it: It's an exceptional experience, really different from what we have seen in the rest of the world. New habits, new courtoisie, it feels so good to be lost in Japan! http://www.kansuiro.co.jp/eng/.

In Hakone there is a pastry house offering such delicious pastries. (I don't remember the name but they also have it at the hotel.)

In Gora village you can climb up the mountain to see the mountain lake, or walk down the hill to the Sculpture Garden (The Hakone Open-air Museum), a beautiful landscape with a permanent open air exhibition of contemporary art from all over the world.

For the ones who love to explore the traces of the past, stop by the Fujiya Hotel, and order a "French potage": It has exactly the same taste as the french potage of my childhood. Nowadays it's rare to find such delicious potage even in France! The reason, why you find french potage in this hotel, is that in the 20s this hotel was the residence of foreign visitors and some of the recipes have been kept from that time. I think Charlie Chaplin was familiar with this place. I recommand to go and visit this hotel only for its french potage and for its nostalgia.

Hakone
Kanagawa

Kansuiro Ryokan has a history of over 400 years, which was formerly called the Motoyu hot springs. The building of Kansuiro has been designated as a heritage building and registered as a prized Cultural Property of Japan.

Henry Scott-Stokes, U.K.

recommends: **Kyoto**

Journalist who has been the Tokyo bureau chief for The Financial Times, The Times and The New York Times.

Length of stay: since 1964 Tokyo Olympics

Where I would like to guide friends visiting Japan, let me name one selection, among the many possibilities: I choose the stone gardens of Kyoto, in particular. These stone gardens are very beautiful. There is a fine book, written by Stephen Mansfield with text and photos by him.

I recommend that a visitor to Japan head straight for Kyoto, if time is limited, and book a room at Tawaraya in Kyoto. They speak English at Tawaraya. The visitor should ask Tawaraya to book a taxi with an English speaking driver to visit stone gardens such as the Ryoan-ji Temple, which is famous, and also little gardens that are not well known at all. These stone gardens with their basic color schemes of gray-white, bright green and black are among the wonders of the world.

Editor's memo   Ryoan-ji : Zen temple with a famous garden

Located in Kyoto's northwest area, the The Rinzai Zen temple Ryoan-ji – Temple of the Peaceful Dragon – was built in the late 1400s, and the garden may be nearly as old. It is best known for its "Karesansui" Zen stone garden, a simple gravel-and-stone arrangement that inspires peace and contemplation. The Zen garden is a collection of 15 rocks, placed in a landscape of raked, white sand. Nowadays a great number of foreign tourist visit this temple.

Ryoan-ji, Photo from the book titled "Japanese Stone Gardens" by Stephen Mansfield published in 2009 by Tuttle in Tokyo.

Im Ho, Korea

recommends:
Kurume in Fukuoka

Korean actor who has played in a number of TV dramas and movies. He often performs in historical dramas that are popular in Asian countries.

Number of visits: 10 times

I would like to recommend going to the very safest city, Kurume. The reason why I recommend this city is not only because it is safe but also because there are a lot of warm-hearted people living in Kurume. When there are kind-hearted people, there will be an atmosphere of warmth and also when there is an atmosphere of warmth, there will be an overflow of their smiles. Plus, it naturally makes food pretty tasty. People who eat wonderful food have leeway in their life and become kind. I personally recommend the city of Kurume, because it is safe, people are kind and the food is delicious.

After I finished an autograph-signing session in Fukuoka, I was introduced to Kurume by visiting my brother, Shinichi Tsukamoto, who lives there. Every place I went, the Kurume City president of the municipal assembly, the director of St. Maria hospital, civil servants and citizens all welcomed me with smiles so I feel like Kurume is a home away from home for me.

The pork ramen soup originated by "Taiho" ramen was very invigorating and healthy, and reduced my feelings of tiredness from my full schedule. Also, I was able to feel the passion of the managing chef of the best Yakitori restaurant "Teppo," which is a cart bar. One of the remarkable things is that on the way back to my hotel, I found "an unknown" cart bar and got out of a taxi and visited the shop. The atmosphere of the cart bar was strange. However, although it was an old structure, it was soft and romantic for some reason and soon I was captivated by the mood. One more surprising thing I discovered after I got to the bar was that most of the dish were Italian. There was Pollack roe pasta, homemade hamburgers, among other dishes, which were all beyond my imagination. I eventually became friends with the manager of the bar and continue to keep in touch with him to this day.

In Korea, the spring rain is at its peak. Whenever rainwater hits car windows, I want to turn the steering wheel and go to the cart shop in Kurume. If you want to experience the most delicious and romantic Pollack roe pasta, just get a ticket to Fukuoka and run to Kurume without hesitation, where there are kind-hearted people and delicious foods waiting for you.

Yakitori Restaurant Teppo's in Hanabatake (branch) in Kurume.

Photo by Hideo Oida

Jake Shimabukuro, U.S.A.

recommends: **Hokkaido**

World renowned ukulele virtuoso known for his inventive styles in jazz, rock, classical, traditional Hawaiian, folk, and flameco.

Number of visits: regularly for his tour.

Hokkaido has always been one of my favorite places to visit when I tour Japan. Hokkaido is known for its amazingly breathtaking scenery. It has some of the most beautiful and lush forests and parks I have ever seen. Taking a walk through the city is always a great way to wind down after an exciting concert. It's a definite "must visit" for any nature lover. Hokkaido is also well known for its delicious seafood. *Ikura* is one of my favorite foods, and Hokkaido is definitely THE place to get the freshest ikura in Japan.

Editor's memo   Northern spacious land with Ainu culture

Hokkaido, the northernmost island of Japan, is dry with low humidity. There remains untouched majestic nature, which attracts a lot of domestic and foreign tourists. Plenty of great food, including seafood and dairy products, is something that draws peoples to the island with 78,521 sq km.

There are many crowd-pleasing tourist spots in Hokkaido such as Sapporo, the capital of Hokkaido; Hakodate, a historic town; Niseko, a popular ski town; Furano and Kushiro, two regions full of nature.

The Ainu, an indigenous people, had lived in Hokkaido even before the Japanese set foot on the island. These people have lived with their gods and obeyed the natural law. Many facilities in Hokkaido aim to preserve and convey their cultural assets.

Japanese crane at Kushiro Moor in Eastern Hokkaido.

Photo by Manabu Matsunaga

Jane Birkin, U.K. / France

recommends:

Sites and scenes around Japan

**Actress and singer known as the muse of Serge Gains-
bourg, who wrote several of her albums, and for her
work on screen collaborating with directors.**

Number of visits: often for more than 40 years

I have visited Japan for more than 40 years! I first went there with
Serge Gainsbourg for the opening of the film "Cannabis" when I was
7 months pregnant with Charlotte! Since then COUNTLESS other
times for song festivals, film festivals, and since "Baby Alone in Babylon,"
for concerts not only in Tokyo but all over Japan. When Serge died, I went
back for the "Casino de Paris" show, when "L'aquoiboniste" was chosen as
the signature song for a TV series and I became number ONE foreign sales
singer in Japan for six months, beating Elton John as I said to my mother.
This was thanks to an ex-producer for Phonogram who came up with the
idea, and to a Frenchman named Francois Dumas who invited Serge and
me to sing in Japan.

My friend Sachiko Nakanishi then brought me over with "Les Visit-
eurs du Soir" for the show "Arabesque" in Japan, with "Conversation" and
I went back with her about ten times for every subsequent show! I have a
LIST of WONDERFUL places, which, with Sachiko's help, I have made.

I took my mother, my daughter Lou, my step-child, and my ex-hus-
band Doillon to a LOVELY spa, Jigokudani. My mother wanted to see
snow monkeys ever since she'd seen an American "Life" magazine cover
thirty years before! Fantastic baths at night snow monkeys in sulfur pools
never to forget, thanks to Duma's wife who's Japanese ONLY Japanese
know this place, very UNFLAH and authentic.

Jigokudani
Nagano

Jigokudani Onsen in Nagano Prefecture is one of Japan's most popular hot springs, whose name is derived for the image of hell it conjures, no doubt due to the boiling water. The onsen is best known for wild Nihon-zaru (Japanese monkeys) soaking in them as the photo above shows. Please note that the onsen can only be reached by foot.

Kyoto with Lou (my daughter when she was about six.), a little wooden hotel in Kyoto where we slept on the floor, DIVINE ... little riverside restaurants, running *geishas* in the night, exoticism, wonder, the temples, the GARDENS, the BEAUTY, the big enclosed Buddha at Nara, the park where the deers ate my yens in my pocket! The cemetery where cigarettes and little glasses of sake were on the graves for a Buddhist's festival for the dead. I'd thought Serge was there as a ghost. Kamakura's great out door Buddha, and Sachiko's mother's fresh tofu!

I recommend Tokyo, too. Dear "Agnes" hotel in the KAGURAZAKA quarter, the whole "quartier" very pretty, lovely shops (very French), boutiques for sandals, plates, cups, green tea, a little like St Germain (in Paris), or Chelsea (in London), so full of charm, Japanese charm, Natsuno for baguettes, old kimonos, wondrous silk suspensions of animals and "good luck" dangling creatures, hand made, wonderful presents. Omotesando, "Nest" fashion boutique, where the beautiful girl GAVE me her jacket, because I admired it, and there were no more. She left it on my dressing room sofa, without a word, SO Japanese, it couldn't happen anywhere else.

A big department store Takashimaya in Nihonbashi quarter, for casseroles Japanese cooking things knives, and my scarf, *Furoshiki*, that is actually a traditional silk little packaging tissue. The Shinjuku Golden Gai at Shinjuku... tiny little bars, sometimes for a capacity of SIX! They KEEP your bottle, it's quite amazing to look at these hundreds of little bars like in an old film ... and at 4:00 A.M. the fish market!

I think I've put in so many stories, my mother and the snow monkeys, the KINDNESS of the people, the CARING is maybe why my feelings are so deep for Japan. In ALL the shops I've mentioned, in every restaurant and boutique , one comes upon such gentleness to strangers. If you go NOW in their hour of need you'll never forget THAT welcome... Since I slept in the little old hotel in Kyoto, with my little daughter Lou, the Japanese culture, the making of the bed, the wooden bath, it's just such wondrous memories and unlike anything in the world. The contemplation at the gardens, the white "wishes" papers at the temples, the children's uniforms, little sailor suits for girls, brass buttons for boys. The Japanese are sensitive and modest, emotion JUST near the skin, and especially now, it's the right time to visit and get to know them.

Nara Park is a large public park located in the heart of the city, at the foot of Mount Wakakusa. The icon of the park is the wild deer, numbering about 1,200. The animal regarded as the gods' messenger in Shinto, roaming freely around the park. The deer have inhabited the area since ancient times and are protected as Natural Monuments by the government.

Janice Tay, Singapore

recommends:

Kyoto

Columnist for The Straits Times, the most widely read newspaper in Singapore. Based in Kyoto, Janice is working on a book about the city.

Length of stay: 4 years

Go see the temple, they tell you: just about every guide to Kyoto will put Kiyomizu-dera near the top of the list of places to visit.

Thousands climb up to the temple each year for the cherry trees in spring and the maple leaves in autumn. But not everyone will notice the shrine behind the main hall where a high-stakes drama is played out regardless of season.

A shrine devoted to love and match-making, Jishu-jinja has two rocks positioned about 25 paces apart. It's said that if you can walk from one to the other with your eyes closed and your mind on your love, all will go well. If you accept directions, you will need an intermediary.

The distance between the two rocks doesn't seem like much but without sight and under pressure, it must feel like a mile.

A woman inches forward, creeping sideways like a crab. About halfway across, she crashes into another supplicant, eyes also shut, approaching from the other rock.

Others end up in front of the souvenir shop or bump against those not watching and grinning.

A girl visiting with her schoolmates decides to brave the journey. She takes the first hesitant steps, her arms stretched out in front of her. One of the boys in her group plonks himself in her path – and waits.

No one warns her because we're all in on the conspiracy.

Jishu-jinja Shrine
Kyoto

地主神社

恋占いの石

The tiny Jishu-jinja is hidden behind the main hall of Kiyomizu-dera, one of the most famous temples in Kyoto. At the shrine, two rocks adorned with sacred rope and paper are located about 25 paces apart. It is said that those who can walk from one rock to the other with their eyes shut and their mind on their beloved will have a successful relationship.

She stumbles into the boy, her arms closing around him. Her eyes fly open; she screams and starts smacking him, in that doggy-paddle scrabbling young women use when they're more interested in high-speed rebuke than in actual maiming.

He laughs as he wards off the blows but doesn't seem the least bit repentant. He's got her attention.

A foreigner in faded jeans is next. His legs are long; even with his eyes closed, he strides. And when his shoe hits the rock on the other side, he hooks his arm around the waiting woman and pulls her in for a kiss.

Strangers applaud. At Jishu-jinja in Kyoto, triumph in a matter as private as love becomes shared celebration.

Editor's memo   Historic, cultural, quiet and beautiful city

Kyoto, a historic city in the Kansai region, is one of the most popular destinations in Japan for both domestic and international tourists. As the country's capital for more than a thousand years, it has amassed a dazzling array of cultural treasures. These range from 17 World Heritage sites, such as Kiyomizu-dera and

Kiyomizu-dera

Nijo Castle, to stunning temple gardens and shops that have maintained their traditions for generations.

There are tons of sites worth recommending but do visit at least one or two of the ancient temples and the Gion district for its geisha and traditional architecture. And don't leave without trying Kyoto's cuisine, said to be among the most refined in Japan.

Jason Wu, U.S.A.

recommends:

Tokyo

Fashion designer known for his beautifully crafted clothes and couture take on sportswear. He counts US First Lady Michelle Obama among his clients.

Number of visits: many times

I stayed in Japan when I was a student and have visited Japan many times since then. It is one of my favorite places to visit for inspiration. I always love getting a crepe in Harajuku, and I love shopping at Designworks.

I love Tokyo; I consistently find inspiration for my collections when I visit. The city is so powerful and energetic, and I often find many ideas by just walking on the streets. Harajuku and Aoyama are two of my favorite parts of Tokyo to visit and shop. I am also obsessed with the various types of Japanese street foods such as *okonomyaki* and *takoyaki*.

Editor's memo   Walk the street, find something new and interesting

There's so much to see on the streets of Tokyo that you could spend days doing just that.

The Harajuku area is a great place to start. At the heart of the action is Takeshi-ta-dori, a street of shops targeting trendy teens. On Sundays, young people dressed up to jaw-dropping extremes pack the area. Grab a crepe from one of the area's many stands and gawk away.

But in nearby Aoyama, the fashion is high-end and the cuisine, exclusive. Even if you've no interest in brand-name boutiques, why not treat yourself to lunch at one of the gourmet restaurants there?

Jean-Philippe Delhomme, France
recommends: **Walking in Tokyo**

Illustrator and writer mainly focusing on the subject of culture, from design and architecture, to fashion or contemporary art.

....

Number of visits: 12 or 15 times since the early 1990's

Photo by Garance Dor .A Ni. With best regards, Jean-Philippe Delhomme

I always loved to walk in Tokyo. Not necessarily through the most famous streets with all the flagship stores, but more the back alleys, the quiet residential or less popular areas. Anything outside the usual path.

To me, the most interesting thing is to visit people or friends at their studios and work spaces: Akira Onozuka from Zucca, the founders of Groovisions, or the young designers of Hirocoledge.

I was taken once on a tour of Modernist Architecture by Casa Brutus which is one of my best memories, from the Museum of Modern Art, Kamakura & Hayama in Kamakura, the Le Corbusier designed the National Museum of Western Art in Tokyo, or Bunka Kaikan (which I heard had been damaged by the earthquake).

I also went to visit Kodokan several times, the great place where Judo was founded and is still taught.

I remember once going through such a lovely flower street market near Asakusa.

And on my last trip, I discovered the Second Hand Bookshops area.

I somehow always felt "at home" and comfortable in Tokyo. I always found there to be a certain dreamy atmosphere, from high rise hotel rooms where you feel like you're floating above the city, to small temple gardens, or wild grass and plants growing along a railroad track. This particular atmosphere melting together the most contemporary architecture of sky-scrapers and the traditional small scale houses, and nature growing at the edge of temporary vacant lots, or in the gardens and roofs is best shown in and embodied by Takashi Homma photographs.

I always saw something very poetic about Tokyo. The pale blue summer skies with those giant white clouds slowly moving far above. The constant extreme between anonymous international flagship stores and buildings, and the intimate tiny places where you might end up with friends at night for a meal or drink, and feel protected as in a peaceful center of the world.

Jimbocho, in Tokyo, is famous as one of the world's largest second-hand book store districts . Each store is small and has its own features such as literature, history, social science, art, sports, classics, and more. There are over 170 bookstores including 52 second-hand book stores in Jimbocho.

Jean Snow, Canada

recommends:

Aoyama district in Tokyo

Writer who lives and breathes design, pop culture, and gaming in Tokyo. He has reported on these obsessions for many online/offline publications.

Length of stay: over 10 years.

For anyone who is interested in experiencing the style and design of Tokyo, I would recommend spending some time in the Aoyama district and in Omotesando. Encountering everything from great fashion and design-related shops to little art galleries and stylish cafes, it's a terrific area to simply wander around, to head down tiny streets that soon reveal hidden treasures.

One of the things that helped kick start my writing career was the love I developed for Japanese art and design, and a lot of my discoveries came from spending time in Aoyama, as well as some of the other nearby districts, like Harajuku, Shibuya, and Daikanyama. Entering shops is like entering a beautifully curated museum or gallery, with innovative design on display everywhere. And because most of these shop owners are so great at finding the best in whatever category of product they are interested in, you really get to see the best the world has to offer.

But more than just the shopping, you are also able to take in some of the most innovative interior design as well, with spaces that act as much as a draw as whatever you find inside. It's certainly a wonderful area to spend some time in, and when you are tired from all the walking around, there's no lack of cafes and restaurants to stop and relax in.

Omotesando
Tokyo

Omotesando is known as a zelkova tree-lined shopping street with many fashion brands outlets in a stylish atmosphere. Currently, Omotesando district exudes an image of high-fashion due to a wave of openings of luxury brands boutiques (but minor brands and low-priced brands also open outlets there).

Jean Touitou, France

recommends:
various spots in Tokyo

Founder and Designer of A.P.C. (Atelier de Production et de Creation), a French fashion brand established in 1987.

Number of visits: on regular bases since 1991

Restaurant TORA* on the underground level of Roppongi Hills Hillside: minimalist yet very tasty grilled food. Perfect after a long flight. No bull shit with attitude and decor. Just the perfect food.

• BAR ROUGE: for the sound of the ice balls (the bar enders sculpt them) in the glass of the perfect cocktail they are in. Those guys are the samurais of the dry martini.

• TANAKA-YA, 5-48-6 JINGUMAE Shibuya-ku: this shop has crafty tea pots, cups, and chandeliers that I have not seen elsewhere in Japan.

• MONTOAK cafe and restaurant: food at any time, relaxing, laid back and trendy at any time. Good for any type of meeting, including business, so you don't have to suicide in hotel lobbies

• Roppongi Hills Aoyama Book Center (ABC): open very late, good books, and even has an excellent supermarket that is open "25 hours a day" I could never figure out what the hell that means.

• MAISEN tonkatsu restaurant: it's a hard drug place. The heroin of pork filet. I'm glad I don't have it near me in Paris.

• TACHIMICHI-YA, B1F 30-8 Sarugaku-cyo, Shibuya-ku: in front of the venue we played at with "Housse de Racket." Japanese food with very loud music. The boss is like John Bellucci turned Japanese.

• SANTA MONICA: vintage denim shop on Omotesando. Very good stuff to grab for the summer season.

Roppongi Hills
Tokyo

One of the Roppongi district's notable landmarks, Roppongi Hills opened in the spring of 2003. It is a rather conventional urban complex, containing offices, shops, restaurants, gardens, walkways, movie theatres, and more. There are also upscale residences for Japanese celebrities.

*TORA Roppongi Hills is now closed. TORA Ebisu is available.

Jihyo Lee, Korea

recommends:
Kochi in Shikoku

1997 Miss Korea - International Director of [The Super Model] Asian Beauty Contest 2011 and Fashion events in Asia.

Length of stay: about 6 years

When the tsunami hit the northern part of Japan, the whole country seemed to feel numb. All we could do was stay glued to the TV for the latest news and what we had to do in an emergency. The aftershocks that followed in downtown Tokyo had the entire population out on the streets, watching the buildings move from side to side. Helpless, just waiting, hanging on the every word of the powers that be as to what our future held.

Like many other families in Japan we decided to head south away from the radiation reach (we still don't know what that is) and strong aftershocks. Some of our family live in the Shikoku region, so we decided to pay them a visit that was long overdue.

When thinking about Japan, people often have an image of the bright lights of Shinjuku, Hachiko crossing in Shibuya or even the distant shot of Mount Fuji. To see the real Japan, you really must travel to the more remote and traditional parts to have an authentic look at one of the most beautiful countries in the world. One of my personal favorites is the island of Kochi in the Shikoku region.

The city is small, with a population under 400,000 people. The local people are very friendly and somehow are able to create a very casual atmosphere wherever you are, which all the shops and local traditions still maintain the character of the south. There is the ever alluring Mt. Go-

Katsurahama Beach
Kochi

Katsurahama is a beautiful beach on the Pacific Ocean located 30 minutes by bus from Kochi Station. There, you will find a statue of the gallant Sakamoto Ryoma (1835-1867), a heroic visionary, facing the beach.

dai, Chikurin-ji Temple (extremely popular with pilgrims) and the most famous Kochi Castle, which dates from back in the feudal period, in the downtown district. If you are more of a seaside person, a must visit is Katsurahama Beach, where you can always engage with a mass of Japan's most enthusiastic surfers and eat a wide variety of barbecued seafood. If you are lucky enough to travel there in the summer you will be able to witness the Yosakoi Festival which boasts thousands of dancers and performers.

The old-style tram will take you through the downtown of the city to one of my favourite stops: that of the most outstanding market called Hirome Ichiba. It is a very open market that encourages families and the young people in the area to mix with each other and features open-style izakaya's, huge sushi bars, soba restaurants and authentic *okonomiyaki* stalls. The most famous food from the area (and a personal favourite of mine) is Katsuo Tataki, a simple fillet of Katsuo which has been lightly seared on all sides (leaving the inside white) and marinated in a local sauce.

Kochi is also the proud home of Sakamoto Ryoma who played a significant role as a Samurai in the Meiji Restoration and is a well-known symbol of that era throughout Japan. After seeing the sights of the area and taking in the various traditions of the area, no trip to Japan would be complete without visiting one of its hot springs. In Kochi, I recommend the Sansuien Onsen, a huge complex that can cater to your every whim with it be the various spa rooms,(inside and outside), the gardens, massage rooms and so on. This place really has it all and is worth the trip alone.

Kochi is another great part of Japan that is rarely seen by visitors. Not only does it have many things to do and see steeped in tradition but most of all it is the warmth of the people that really make you want to come back again.

John
J. Boccellari, U.S.A.
recommends: **Kii Peninsula**

Professor, Graduate School of Arts and Sciences, Department of Comparative Literature and Culture, University of Tokyo

Length of stay: 41 years

I have lived in Japan for 41years. I would recommend the beautiful scenic and religious sites of the Kii Peninsula.

Ise, Kumano, Koya-san all have something to do with "rebirth" and "rejuvenation". The whole area is a beautiful reminder that Japanese culture developed through a dialogue between the mountains and the sea. The Peninsula is a promise from nature that the Japanese people will survive and prosper despite any challenge, natural or otherwise, that may arise.

Editor's memo   Ancient pilgrimage road is now a world heritage site

The Kii Peninsula is a large peninsula in south central Honshu, that juts into the Pacific Ocean to the south and the Inland Sea to the west. In 2004, the Kumano's religious treasures and the routes, including Koyasan and Yoshino areas in the peninsula, were registered as a UNESCO World Cultural Heritage Site.

Kumano Kodo

Jonathan Barnbrook, U.K.

recommends: **Hiroshima**

Graphic designer working from London. His studio designed the CI's for Roppongi Hills, Daichi Wo Mamoru Kai, collaborating with artists such as Damien Hirst.

Number of visits: on a regular basis for 15 years

Why am I suggesting to go to a place associated with 'the nuclear' when Japan is trying to move on from the tsunami, earthquake, and nuclear meltdown? Because after the recent earthquake the context of Hiroshima changed. Before you visit the museum, there is something else about Hiroshima that you will see. The city will always be identified with the atomic bomb, but life has moved on for the people. There are children happily cycling from school, lush green grass covering public spaces, motorists getting angry about traffic jams, and people laughing in the streets. If the people of Hiroshima can overcome and become concerned with the business of living again, then we know that the recent problems in Japan can be dealt with and got over. Loss is a real physical pain, but time heals, people are resilient, they recover, fall in love again, build their business, feel optimistic and have hope about the future. Hiroshima is a positive and poignant reminder of what is possible.

Once you are inside the Hiroshima Peace Memorial Museum, the mood is very different. Displayed are the atrocious photographs which have all been burned into our eyes from the moment at school we heard that man was capable of creating such a weapon. Even more terrible are the children's drawings at the time, laden with emotional intensity and a naive misunderstanding of why this happened that no camera can capture.

A-Bomb Dome
Hiroshima

Hiroshima Peace Memorial Park, locating in central Hiroshima City. Completed in 1954, the park contains a total of 66 statues, monuments, and buildings, and stands as a symbol of the nuclear abolition movement and the vow of the human race to pursue peace.

But there is another equally overwhelming transitional human experience, through the 'poetic' understanding of the fleeting nature of our own existence that comes through unconsciously when you walk around the museum. In several watches and clocks on display that stopped at the time the atomic bomb detonated, at the moment the people's lives stopped, we see that we all have our own internal clock, ticking away to its end. This confirms our own limited time, reminds us to make use of it more. Later on and most incredible for me in the exhibition, the 'intangible' has been captured, the shadow of a human being, caught in the brilliant heat of the explosion. This negative 'space' is now physical – the shadow – a subject of myths, ghost stories, representation of the other side of our personality – is now the only thing left of a living, breathing human being, and yet it shows us that our own lives are mere shadows, flickering for 70 years across the earth and we are gone. We must live, laugh, celebrate, let those around us know how much we love them, reconcile with old enemies, be a more useful citizen, make use of this wonderful gift of life that we have, forget the petty frustrations and live to our potential as humans.

Editor's memo   Hiroshima: City of Peace

Facing the Seto Inland Sea, Hiroshima is the largest city in the Chugoku region of Honshu. The city flourished as a castle town after Mouri Terumoto, a feudal lord, built Hiroshima Castle in 16th century. At 8:15 A.M. on August 6, 1945, the first atomic bomb ever used against humankind fell on Hiroshima. With a blinding flash and a deafening roar, a single bomb instantly destroyed the city beyond recognition.

Hiroshima Castle

Today Hiroshima is known as the "City of Peace". Numerous tourist-favored destinations include the Hiroshima Castle, Shukkei-en Garden, the Mitaki-dera Temple, and the Hiroshima Peace Memorial (the Atomic Bomb Dome).

Children's Peace Monument, completed on May 5, 1958 (Children's Day in Japan). It was established by the Hiroshima Society of School Children for Building World Peace. On the stone underneath the pedestal is inscribed, "This is our cry. This is our prayer. For building peace in this world."

Karel van Wolferen, Netherlands

recommends: **Oirase Valley**

Author who used to be a foreign correspondent for East Asia, based in Tokyo. Nowadays he write books and articles.

Length of stay: more than 35 years, and still visits

I could recommend almost any place in Japan, both for its scenic beauty and the pleasure of being among Japanese people. I have travelled almost everywhere in Japan and have never been disappointed. In a kind of second life, I am a large-format landscape photographer, and Japan is perfect for that purpose with its incredibly beautiful sceneries.

Let me just mention a few places that stand out and where I have been in recent years. The mountain areas of Tohoku are a must, but to see them at their best you must travel by car. The Oirase Valley in Aomori Prefecture is great, especially in autumn. Winter in the mountains of Hokkaido can be extraordinarily spectacular.

For an easier trip nearer Tokyo that can be done in one day, one should go to Mt. Mitake, west of Tokyo. You can also stay at the lovely little Komadori Sanso at the top, near the shrine. Beautiful surroundings in every season. A bit farther, Nagano and Gifu Prefectures are marvelous destinations. Take Route 98, between Gero and Takayama up to the 48 waterfalls park (Shiju-hattaki Kougen).

Recently, my wife and I have greatly enjoyed Matsumoto and Takayama. There are great *izakayas* near the station in Matsumoto in Nagano. Of course, there are great izakaya's almost everywhere in Japan. Another spot in that area is Asama Onsen, especially its lovely old-fashioned Sakae No Yu Ryokan. It's a perfect spot for a lazy read at the end of a day spent driving over mountain roads.

Oirase
Aomori

Oirase Stream, a striking, picturesque mountain stream which runs through Oirase Valley in Aomori Prefecture. It is one of the best known and popular autumn color sites in Japan and has plenty of water with over a dozen waterfalls cascading down the walls of the gorge all along its length.

Train travel is obviously efficient in Japan, and I would recommend going to a hub station and taking local trains from there to rural areas. Still, it is worthwhile for even a short-term visitor to rent a car and see the nooks and crannies of mountain areas with small *ryokan*. In that way you will see shrines whose existence you would never have guessed and meet people you will never forget.

I recently took a wrong turn in Yamanashi Prefecture and discovered country roads that brought memories back of a Japan that I had known in the 1960s. It is possible to take just one prefecture, not even one that is famous for its scenery, and spend a week exploring its details.

Getting lost is no problem; in fact it offers opportunities that one would otherwise not have to see things that one would otherwise not see, and to get acquainted with ordinary people with whom you can hardly communicate, but who turn out to be among the most warm-hearted and helpful people you have ever met.

Again, I want to recommend anywhere in Japan. But concerning the places mentioned above, we have had great experiences sitting on the bare floor of a simple *izakaya* with total strangers, who thought that we would miss the best sakes if they did not help us by ordering them.

If you cannot get out of Tokyo, you will probably visit Asakusa. After you have admired the recently restored Asakusa Kannon Temple (Senso-ji), veer off to the left (when facing the temple), walk a few hundred meters and locate the outdoor tables of a variety of *izakaya's*. Nearby, across the Sumida River, in Higashi Komagata, you can visit our favorite *izakaya* called Inagaki – no doubt Tokyo "*shitamachi*" at its best.

If you are stuck in central-central Tokyo, do not miss the huge Beer Hall Lion at Ginza 7-chome, probably the most beautiful art deco interior you have ever seen, totally preserved in its early 20th century state. For a smaller, more intimate place with exquisite fish dishes, visit Shin Hinomoto under the railway arches near Yurakucho Station, and tell Andy, who runs it, that I sent you.

Beer Hall Lion Ginza 7-chome Branch, one of the symbolic restaurants of Ginza. The building inside is unchanged since its opening in 1934.

Lori Matsukawa , U.S.A.

recommends:

Tokyo and Shirakawa-go

News Anchor and reporter for KING 5 TV in Seattle for nearly 30 years. President of the Board of Directors, Japanese Cultural and Community Center of Washington.

Number of visits: 5 times.

My first trip to Japan was in 1973 as part of a high school choir, the Aiea Swinging Singers. We performed a Polynesian show at a Tokyo hotel for nearly a week. My second visit was in 1974 as Miss Teenage America, destination: Tokyo. My third trip to Japan: in 1995 as a reporter for KING 5 TV to cover trade issues in Tokyo and Sendai. My fourth trip to Japan was in 2005 as part of the Japanese American Leadership Delegation. Our delegation visited Tokyo, Kyoto, and Kobe. My latest trip to Japan was in March 2011 for KING 5 TV to cover the aftermath of the Tohoku earthquake and tsunami.

My husband and I are planning a tour of Japan. It would start in Tokyo with a city tour and attending a sumo tournament. We look forward to visiting Shirakawa-go, a UNESCO World Heritage Site. We will also visit the beautiful temples of Kyoto and then head south to Hiroshima.

We would like to experience ancient and modern Japanese architecture and culture and take in the natural beauty of the country. This is the land of my ancestors and we want to connect with my family history. We would not go north of Tokyo in light of the tsunami damage and radiation danger near the Fukushima Daiichi Nuclear plant. And while the radiation levels in food and water may be slightly elevated in Japan, we do not believe it poses an extreme risk to our health. We also want to support the Japanese economy as it rebuilds after the earthquake and tsunami.

Shirakawa-go
Gifu

Shirakawa-go is a village located in the mountain in the north of Gifu prefecture, with a population of about 600. Most of the houses in the village are constructed in a style called *gassho* (literally, "two hands in prayer") *zukuri*, in which houses have steep, thatched roofs forming an "A" shape.

Marc Newson, Australia

recommends:

Tokyo

Designer working across a wide range of disciplines, creating everything from furniture and household objects, to bicycles and cars, private and commercial aircraft etc.

Number of visits: some times

Photo by Romeo Balancout

I would say that Japan is my favorite place to live. I had (and still have) some of the best times of my life in Tokyo, but I also love staying in the mountains in remote parts of the countryside where I do nothing except sit in hot natural thermal baths (onsen) .

I love the everyday aesthetics of Japan. The obsession with detail really impresses me. The Japanese have such a different sense of visual logic.

TOKYO is most definitely my favourite city in the world; I am always excited by the mix of the ancient and traditional with the current craziest pop culture.

Some of my favourite things:

• Japanese Tea - 'Hoji-cha' from Ippodo Tea Shop in Kyoto
• Traditional Japanese incense from Shoyeido in Kyoto
• The Restaurant, Tora Kuma Mogura in Tokyo

My favorite form of architecture in Japan is first and foremost traditional Japanese. The lobby of the Hotel Okura Tokyo is a great example of mid-century modern and I particularly like that space. It is the atmosphere of the space and the way it functions—like a well-oiled machine—rather than the architecture itself that impresses me.

The Okura was built just before the Tokyo Olympics and it still has the atmosphere of the era. Everything in the Okura is clean and ironed.

When I get back to the hotel in the deep of the night after spending time in Roppongi, they are cleaning up public spaces. They are very quiet and perfect. I think it is very Japanese, very Tokyo.

Toranomon
Tokyo

Hotel Okura Tokyo, situated in Toranomon, the heart of downtown Tokyo. The Main Building lobby is known for the soft illumination of the Okura Lantern, which continues to shed light on the lobby, never once being dimmed since the hotel's opening in 1962. Photo provided by Hotel Okura Tokyo.

Mark Borthwick , U.K.

recommends:

Yamanashi

Photographer/artist known for his award winning avant-garde fashion photography.

Number of visits: so many times

Yamanashi, a place that's very dear to my heart because of their collective community, which is inspired through the love of Etsuko Miyoshi who's gallery trax is a very rare place in Japan that collectively brings life together among friends and lovers.

I feel today it seems an odd request to venture people towards the chaos of city life, in the end to define a difference would be to the commercial side of city life therefore her parks and gardens to stream one in towards getting lost with time, so to the country we go.

For there were able to feel the way they have lived traditionally without the needs of consumerism. one's able to find themselves in a new environment where nature there to rape you escape you and let time breath its way away.

Editor's memo   Yamanashi: a prefecture with beautiful nature

Yamanashi is an inland prefecture, located immediately west of Tokyo. Its proud icon is Mount Fuji situated in the south. With 80% of its land covered by forests, Yamanashi abounds with nature: it embraces spectacular 3,000-meter mountain ranges, popular Fuji Five Lakes and beautiful valleys, providing abundant outdoor activities. It has Japan's biggest vineyard producing internationally acclaimed Koshu wine.

Gallery Trax in Hokuto City in Yamanshi Prefecture, photographed by Mark Borthwick. Visit their website for more information about their exhibition at www.eps4.comlink.ne.jp/~trax/frame.html

Matthew Barney, U.S.A.

recommends:

Yakushima Island in Kyushu

Artist who works in sculpture, photography, drawing and film. His early works were sculptural installations combined with performance and video.

Number of visits: 6 or 7 times.

I have visited Japan six or seven times over the years, most extensively in 2004/2005.

My favorite site is Yakushima, an island to the south of Kyushu in Kagoshima Prefecture.

The deities on this island are 3,000-year-old Yakusugi Cedar trees. To see these ancient trees you'll need to hike into the center of the island, to elevations above 1,000 meters, where it is densely forested and extremely humid. Along the way, you will see dwarf *shika* deer, macaque monkeys, and sections of the forest completely engulfed in moss. It is beautiful.

Editor's memo   The Island of Mountains with preserved nature

Yakushima is an island off the southeast coast of Kyushu next to Tanegashima and north of Okinawa. It is home to a huge cedar forest that contains some of Japan's oldest living trees, known as Yakusugi, among the oldest of which is Jomonsugi, believed to be around 7,000 years old. Also, there are a number of mountains such as Mt. Miyanoura-dake and Mt. Nagata-dake. Yakushima served as a model forest for the renowned animated movie "Princess Mononoke" by Hayao Miyazaki and is designated as a UNESCO World Heritage Site.

Shiratani Unsuikyo is a popular sightseeing destination in Yakushima Island, where is a park of yakusugi, or island's ancient cedars. Visitors can see the forest without a strenuous hike there.

Yakushima
Kagoshima

Magnificently enormous Yakushima Jomonsugi is the oldest and largest cedar tree on the island, a UNESCO World Heritage Site in Japan, and is estimated to be between 2,170 and 7,200 years old.

Neville Brody, U.K.

recommends:

Spots in Tokyo

Creative Director of Research Studios and Dean of Communication Art & Design, Royal College of Art.

Number of visits: every year and stay for a week

(c) Akemi Kurosaka 2010

I've been fortunate to visit Japan many times and also travel the country on business but there is still something so unique about Tokyo that I am always drawn back, especially with my son who has taken holiday with me there several times and loves it too.

For everyone that goes to Tokyo I tell them to expect the unexpected as it's a great city where everything feels familiar but at the same time unfamiliar. In no particular order I've put together a random list of places that I think make this city so unique.

Shibuya is my favorite place to stay. It's the heart of the young community and alive 24/7. Hachiko crossing is an experience you would struggle to find anywhere else in the world, with thousands of people crossing the road at one time and the odd lost tourist totally overloaded by the experience.

Tokyu Hands is the best store on earth. It has everything that you need and don't need, and a thousand types of every item. The Shibuya branch is a massive store that you can get lost in for at least half a day, I visit on every trip.

Montoak on Omotesando is great for its lunchtime Bento boxes with a certain European sensibility. For something more comforting and a Tokyo institution you can't go wrong with Maisen's pork Katsu also in Omotesando.

Akihabara is the electronics mecca of Tokyo. Literally buzzing with energy, it's a one-stop shop for not only electronics and computer goods, but also anime and *otaku* too. It's a great place to pick up "Gundam" to add to my collection.

Ginza Graphic Gallery has hosted several of my own exhibitions and I always return for a dose of graphic design or illustration inspiration. I love their book series.

Kiddy Land is another 'full-on' shopping experience as local and international children (with their parents in tow) spend small fortunes on toys of all shapes, sizes, and characters.

In Akihabara, a town famous for anime and electronics, visitors might catch a glimpse of women dressed in uniforms just like in this photo.

Pan Qing Lin, China

recommends:

Kyoto

Chinese Politician who has devoted to bridge between China and Japan.

Number of visits: many times

It was 25 years ago when I came to Japan for the first time. I was a student and soon found living in Japan interesting—scenic views, delicious cuisines, and the culture of its so-called Yamato people, the majority of Japanese.

While I had some hardships, I also got an opportunity to have good education in Japan. Thanks to those experiences, today I am a congressional representative of China. I married a Japanese woman, and Japan is my adopted home.

I went to and from China and Japan for many years and continued my businesses and studies. I was very busy, though I enjoyed traveling around Japan, and its beautiful sceneries. Thus, I was able to understand the Japan's exotic and esoteric culture and the spirit of the people of Japan. I also made many Japanese friends from various fields and learned some regional traditions and customs.

Among many recommended sites such as Hokkaido, Mt. Fuji, and Okinawa, the most influential one on me was Kyoto. The beautiful view of Kyoto features 17 World Heritage Sites; spring cherry and autumnal leaf coloration are internationally famous and popular. Additionally, I was moved by its culture. Kyoto has a long history, conveying the culture and tradition of thousands of years and expressing the wisdom and the essence of Japanese people.

We can see the architectures established a thousand years ago. To my surprise, not only the buildings are preserved, but also traditions and culture of the ancient days have also been passed on. I was fascinated ancient books and musical instruments and when I stepped into the Kinkaku-ji Temple (Golden Pavilion), I felt as if I transcended time and space into the shining ancient period.

Nowadays, there are historic and modern cultures coexisting in Japan; kimono and modern fashion depict the sense of peace. The advanced spinning and weaving technology and highly elaborated artifacts contributed to the Japanese economy. Succeeding the Japanese hardworking spirit and pursuing the passion for the future, Japan will not bow to any natural disaster but get over it, I believe. I cheer for Japan. Go for it, Japan!

Kinkaku-ji
Kyoto

Kinkaku-ji, officially named Rokuon-ji, is perhaps the most famous site in Kyoto. It was originally established as a villa in 1224 and, in the 14th century, Ashikaga Yoshimitsu, the third shogun of the Ashikaga shogunate during the Muromachi period, took possession of the villa for his retirement.

Paul Smith, U.K.

recommends:

Tsumago and Magome

Fashion designer, renowned for his idiosyncratic take on traditional British styling-classics with a twist. He combines commercial success with critical credibility.

Number of visits: more than 80 times since 1982

In Tokyo, I would suggest visiting Shibuya for its variety of stores, restaurants, and Aoyama/Harajuku where there are a lot of fashion shops, ranging from high-end to very local and small, as well as vintage.

In countryside, I would suggest Magome and Tsumago villages, where tradition, old houses and old streets still exist.

I used to visit country side personally when I started my business in Japan about 30 years ago, but now I really don't have enough time to visit apart from Tokyo where I am only allowed to walk around near my office in Aoyama, Harajuku and Shibuya due to my busy schedule. However, I always find some new interesting things and like watching people, how they dress etc.

I was lucky to have time to visit Tsumago and Magome for a project with a magazine last year, and I found these villages are so beautiful. It is great to see that they are still there and unchanged, which is rare and amazing!

Editor's memo   Nakasendo's two historic post towns

Tsumago and Magome were post stations located on the Nakasendo Route, which is one of the Gokaido, the five major highways during the Edo Period. The Nakasendo liked Edo and Kyoto through the inland are and had 69 post stations.

Magome
Gifu

Magome in Gifu prefecture

Robert J. Geller, U.S.A.

recommends:

Lake Ashi and Lake Chuzenji

Professor of Geophysics in the School of Science of the University of Tokyo, conducting research on computational methods for modeling the propagation of seismic waves.

Length of stay: since 1984

Actually my wife and I enjoy taking short vacations near Lake Ashi in Hakone and Lake Chuzenji, in the hills above Nikko. We like the "Hôtel de Yama" (http://www.odakyu-hotel.co.jp/yama-hotel/english/) near Lake Ashi, and the Chuzenji Kanaya Hotel (http://www.kanayahotel.co.jp/english/chuzenji/access.html) near Lake Chuzenji. Both are nice quiet hotels with hot spring baths (onsen) and due to the elevation are pleasantly temperate even during the summer.

We are both very busy in our respective jobs in Tokyo, and we like nice, pleasant, quiet places where we can go for a couple of days to relax and unwind. We can soak in the hot spring pools and also take nice walks in the areas around these hotels, where the scenery is natural and rural. Both of these hotels are only a couple of hours from Tokyo by rail and bus. If you're only making a brief visit to Japan you will want to make sure you hit the standard highlights such as Kyoto, but even so you might also enjoy relaxing for a day or so away from the big cities.

Editor's memo   Lake Chuzenji: scenic lake especially in autumn color

Lake Chuzenji was created 20,000 years ago when Mt. Nantai erupted. Its shores are mostly undeveloped and forested except at its eastern end where Chuzenjiko Onsen is.

Lake Ashi
Kanagawa

Surrounded by mountains and dense forest, Ashinoko (Lake Ashi) was formed in the caldera of Mt. Hakone around 3,000 years ago. Today, the Lake, also known as Hakone Lake, is a symbol of Hakone with its beautiful scenery of Mt. Fuji and numerous hot springs. Many sightseeing boats and ferries await visitors.

Sarah, France

recommends:

Tokyo non-stop day and night

Art Director of the Parisian concept store Colette. Defined by four sub-headings: style, design, art and food, Colette has become much more than a shop.

Number of visits: countless times

I first went to Japan when I was 18 and I went there regularly since. During our pop up shop with Comme des Garçons, I went every month !

I like :

• Naoshima in Shikoku: http://www.benesse-artsite.jp/en/about/

• Ginzan Hot spring Fujiya Inn: http://www.fujiya-ginzan.com/

• Coffees-Tea-Drinks: Higashiya, Nara A-Z (Aoyama); Piano Bar (Shibuya)

• Restaurants: Tonki (Meguro); Savoy Pizzeria (Roppongi)

• Bookshops: Cow books; TSUTAYA's Roppongi Hills store.

• Shopps: Kiddyland; Comme des Garçons; OriginalFake, Bonjour Records

• Break: Nezu Museum (Aoyama); Uka Nails (Tokyo Midtown).

Editor's memo   Ginzan Onsen: evoking the atmosphere of old Japan

---

Locating along the Ginzan River in Yamagata, Ginzan Onsen is known as a location used for the filming of "Oshin," a famous Japanese TV drama series that has been broadcast in many countries. You will see graceful three- and four-story wooden inns line both banks of the Ginzan River.

Seung Woo Back, Korea

recommends:
Tokyo

Seoul- based artist working on a number of group and solo project around the world.

Number of visits: one time for a month.

I strongly recommend Tokyo.
Not many reasons--everything is there: People, art, restaurants, architecture, passion, history.....

Ginza
Tokyo

Japan's leading shopping town. The Ginza 4-chome intersection is located at the heart of the shopping district.

Theseus Chan, Singapore

recommends:

Ochanomizu

Creative Director/Designer of WORK and WERK Magazine in Singapore. He was conferred the "Designer of the Year" award at the inaugural President's Design Award.

Number of visits: many times

Photo by Tommy O'Gara

What recommendations would you give to friends who are visiting Tokyo after the great earthquake?

• Fashion: For fashion it is Omotesando in Aoyama area, especially the Comme des Garçons and 10 Corso Como Comme des Garçons stores.

Fashion ideas in Tokyo come and go very quickly, and the retail scene is changing all the time. The discovery of new products, shops and retail innovations is always a delight in this area.

Department stores that go on the "must-visit" list are Seibu Shibuya and Isetan Men's in Shinjuku.

Another delightful area is Ueno, where you will be surprised by the variety of food and vintage American goods available at the Ameyayokocho Black Market. The atmosphere is electric!

• Musical Instruments: Tokyo is also a great place to purchase new and vintage musical instruments, particularly guitars and their peripherals.

For guitar enthusiasts, I would recommend guitar shops in Shibuya and Ochanomizu. The levels of service and knowledge expressed by the staff are true examples of Japanese professionalism. The Ikebe, Ishibashi and Kurosawa stores are definite stops to add on the travel list.

• Accommodation: Serviced apartments are my preferred choice as they are usually situated in residential districts, which I enjoy exploring.

Such accommodations also provide the convenience of home like the kitchen and laundry. I prefer to stay in the Shibuya or Shinjuku neighbourhoods, and I would recommend Hundred Stay as they offer great prices for their facilities.

Guitar shops in Ochanomizu

Tom Heneghan, U.K.

recommends:

The Hokoku-ji Bamboo Garden

Professor of Architecture at Tokyo University of the Arts. His architectural works have received numerous awards, internationally.

Length of stay: 15 years

Although it's best to avoid the areas that were devastated by the earthquake/tsunami - so that the peoples' struggle doesn't become a tourist spectacle - travel in all parts of Japan is easy and very safe. But, my suggestion isn't very adventurous – you don't have to travel far. It's close to Tokyo. And, it's featured on the covers of all tourist guidebooks. It's Kamakura. As a foreigner in Japan you quickly learn that your visit will be more pleasurable if you are prepared to seek delight in different things than you would at home – in un-obvious, or less-obvious, places. As a former capital city, Kamakura has many shrines and temples and sculptures of great beauty and artistry – but I prefer to go, instead, to the less-visited Engaku-ji Temple, the Museum of Modern Art, and the Hokoku-ji Bamboo Garden.

The Hokoku-ji bamboo garden is a thrilling environmental experience, rather than a thing to look at. It may even be at its best in driving rain. Drink green tea in the pavilion, and watch the trees and shadows move in the wind. The Museum of Modern Art was built in 1951, six years after the end of the war, when Japan was absolutely broke. But, somehow, with the cheapest of materials, the young architect Junzo Sakakura was able to conjure a series of simple, beautiful, tranquil experiences. I've seen a photograph of Sakakura showing his former employer, the great Swiss architect Le Corbusier, around the building. Corbusier looks grumpy. Maybe

Kamakura
Kanagawa

Hokoku-ji Temple is considerably new in Kamakura as it was built in 1334, a year after the Kamakura Shogunate came to an end. It is known for the picturesque bamboo forest behind the main road.

because Sakakura's museum is so much more delightful than the great master's own, far more expensive and aloof museum in Tokyo's Ueno Park.

And finally, Engaku-ji. This is where you go to feel, rather than look at Japan's religious architecture. On my first visit there, near the entrance I was intrigued by the sound of repetitive 'thwacks' from behind a tall hedge, and found a 'Kyudo' (Japanese archery) class in progress, led by an extremely ancient monk with long white beard. With a nod, he dispatched a young girl student to wordlessly guide me to a bench, and to light mosquito coils at my feet so that I could enjoy watching the class in comfort. At the end of the lesson the monk hobbled slowly over to the base of the long flight of steps that leads up to the main building, bowed a graceful farewell to me, and…raced up the stairs as if he was a teenager! I think he knew I was still watching.

Editor's memo   Kamakura: 800 years in history with many temples

Kamakura is one of the most popular tourist destinations in Japan, locatied less than an hour south of Tokyo, which itself can not be described without its history. Kamakura became the political center in 1192 when the shogun Minamoto Yoritomo established Bakufu, a military government that ruled Japan for over a century.

Today, the atmosphere of old Japan still remains in Kamakura with its many temples, shrines and other historical monuments, particularly its the Great Buddha Statue (Daibutsu) and Tsurugaoka Hachimangu shrine. Kamakura is surrounded by mountains and beaches, and there are many hiking trails.

Engaku-ji Temple, established by the ruling regent Hojo Tokimune in 1282, is one of the leading temples of Rinzai Sect of Zen Buddhism in eastern Japan and ranks second among Kamakura's five great Zen temples.

Tom Vincent, U.K.

recommends:

Shodoshima Island in Shikoku

CEO at Tonoloop Networks, Inc. working with corporations, organizations and individuals in Japan to bring the best of Japan to the world.

Length of stay: 20 years

I would recommend a visit to the island of Shodoshima, in the Seto Inland Sea.

The Inland Seas is a stretch of water 450 km long, that separates the three main islands of the Japanese Archipelago—Honshu, Shikoku and Kyushu.

The sea is one of Japan's best kept secrets - a stunning, calm expanse of water, dotted with 3,000 islands, big and small, many of which are uninhabited. These islands are home to orange orchards, olive groves, *nori* farms, soy sauce breweries and truly fabulous scenery. This is "Japan's Mediterranean."

Shodoshima is one of the larger of the islands, with a population of around 32,000 people.

Start your journey on the the ferry from Takamatsu, in Kagawa prefecture. An hour or so on the boat is the perfect way to slip into another time-frame, ready for the slow pace of the island.

Once there, you will be able to find traditional *somen* noodle makers - be sure to get there in the morning to see the curtains of yellow noodles drying in the sun. You can also visit traditional and modern soy-sauce breweries. At Yamaroku Shoyu Brewery (http://yama-roku.net/), for example, you can see soy-sauce being made exactly as it has been for over 400 years, climb inside six-foot-wide cedar barrels, and even try some va-

Shodoshima
Kagawa

Angel Road in Shodoshima Island is a sandy stretch connecting the island's mainland at Tonosho with one of the small islands. This stretch is passable on foot twice a day and it is said that couples who cross the sandbar will increase their happiness. Photo provided by Shodoshima Tourist Association

nilla ice-cream with soy-sauce topping. (Sounds weird, I know, but think luxurious caramel!)

Next go for a wander through the olive groves. Shodoshima is Japan's main producer of olives, and you can buy all kinds of products there: foods, creams, as well as shampoos and other cosmetics.

If you have a chance, climb up Mt Goishi. At the top, you'll find a temple built into a natural cave. The views from the summit,, over the harbor and across the Inland Sea to Shikoku, are breath-taking.

And if you are lucky enough to be in Shodoshima on either May 3rd, or October 10th, you will be able to experience one of the biannual *Noson Kabuki* (Farmer's Kabuki theater) shows. These fabulous, traditional open-air theater performances are held in buildings that are over 300 years-old, and are all performed by local farmers and children in a tradition that's been passed down from generation to generation.

There are lots of hotels on Shodoshima, but for a special treat you should stay at Mari, a wonderful family-run inn that is a mix of modern and traditional, with beautifully decorated rooms, and some of the best food on the island, too. http://www.mari.co.jp/

Editor's memo   Beautiful Island with oddly-shaped rocks

Shodoshima Island is situated at the eastern tip of the Bisan Islands, northeast of Takamatsu, Kagawa Prefecture. Thanks to its mild weather, the island enjoys a rich harvest of citrus fruits and olives—In 1908, the island became the first place in Japan to successfully cultivate olives.

Mount Hoshigajo is the highest peak on the island, and Utsukushi-no-hara, a flat plateau expanding out over the west side of this mountain, offers scenic views. Another tourist destinations is Kanka Valley, where you can walk along the promenade, or enjoy the view from the ropeway (aerial tramway) running between steep cliffs.

Shodoshima is also known as the locale of "Nijushi-no-hitomi (Twenty-Four Eyes)," a gentle, sensitive Japanese novel written by Sakae Tsuboi.

Yamaroku Shoyu started its business around 150 years ago. The brewery uses huge cedar barrels and its storehouse is open for visitors to see the process of making Japanese soy sauce.

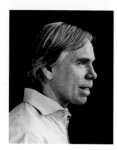

Tommy Hilfiger, U.S.A.

recommends:

Tokyo

Founder and principal designer of Tommy Hilfiger Corporation, a global lifestyle brand with an American spirit. The brand has over 1,000 retail stores across 65 countries.

Number of visits: several times

One of my most memorable trips to Japan was in 2005 for the brand's 20th anniversary. I was thrilled to be able to celebrate such an important milestone in Japan, and was able to visit many of my favorite sites in and around Tokyo.

There are so many things to see and admire in and around Tokyo, but here are a few that I remember being very fond of:

- Meiji-jingu Shrine and Yoyogi Park
- The Mori Art Museum in Roppongi Hills
- Hakusan Ceramics
- The Harajuku district
- Omotesando Road in Aoyama
- Fukuzushi in Roppongi
- Antique markets such as Nogi-jinja Shrine, Togo-jinja Shrine or Hanazono-jinja Shrine

One of my all-time favorite places to visit in Tokyo is Meiji-jingu Shrine, the most important Shinto shrine in all of Tokyo. It is a wonderful place to learn about and appreciate traditional Japanese culture. It's an oasis of calm located in Yoyogi Park in the heart of Tokyo - a nice refuge from the surrounding bright lights of the big city.

I love going the Mori Art Museum in the Roppongi Hills Mori Tower in Tokyo. I find the contemporary art exhibits so inspiring and unique,

Meji-jingu
Tokyo

Meiji-jingu Shrine is a site where people can have Shinto-style wedding parties parade through the inner ground of the shrine. If you're lucky, you will see a bride in traditional Japanese wedding kimono (*Uchikake*), shrine maidens, Shinto priests and a wedding party with women in gorgeous kimono.

and there's always something new to see.

I like to stop by Hakusan, where you can find beautiful ceramics and dinnerware from designer Masahiro Mori. I love the simple designs and bold colors; you can find just the right piece for your home, or to give as a gift.

Harajuku is a mecca for the young, hip and fashionable, and a great place for people-watching. I love to walk through the streets and see how young people are dressed. There is so much creativity! I like to see people put their own spin on fashion.

Omotesando hosts an impressive collection of stores and cafes—there is so much to see! When in Tokyo, I like to walk through the neighborhood to admire boutiques and people-watch.

Sushi is one of my all-time favorite foods, so I always make time to try new sushi restaurants in Tokyo. I like the modern look and bold colors of Fukuzushi, which has delicious sushi. I also love to get recommendations from locals on harder to find, up-and-coming sushi bars.

If you love antiques, I would recommend checking out one of Tokyo's outdoor antique markets, such as Nogi-jinja, Togo-jinja or Hanazono-jinja. There is so much culture and history in these markets, it's fascinating. My daughter Ally loves vintage shopping so I try to bring home something for her that catches my eye.

Editor's memo   Meiji-jingu Shrine: right next to the fashionable Harajuku

----

Following the death of Emperor Meiji in 1912, the Japanese people wished to commemorate his role in the Meiji Restoration (which modernized Japan) and a resolution was passed to build the shrine. The Meiji-jingu is in a quiet and expansive 700,000 square-meter forest with 365 different species of trees (with approximately 100,000 trees donated from across the nation). The shrine grounds consist of two areas, Nai-en and Gai-en. The shrine pavilions are in Nai-en, where tourists can appreciate the harmony of the gravel, the forest and the Shinto architecture.

Tyler Brûlé, Canada

recommends:

Obuse, Kamakura, and Tokyo

Editor in chief of global affairs magazine, Monocle. Creative Director and founder of international branding and design agency, Winkreative.

Number of visits: many times

I've visited six times this year and around once every two months for the last 15 years.

I would send people to Obuse for sake, Kamakura for curry and pancakes and Tokyo for everything else.

My list is endless – the crafts, the food, the cosy neighbourhoods, the lovely people, the service, the ease of travel, ANA, *eki-ben*, late nights shopping at Tsutaya ...

Chestnut Path in Obuse, Nagano Prefecture. The small town blends culture and the arts with an atmosphere of camaraderie, for good food and sake. Katsushika Hokusai, a highly-acclaimed *ukiyo-e* painter, spent his senior years here.

Volker Quandt, Germany

recommends:

Hikone in Shiga

Theater-director of over 60 productions in Germany and in many other countries, including Denmark, Sweden, Brazil, Chile, Ghana and Japan.

Number of visits: almost every year since 1993.

After directing two theater plays in Tokyo back in 1993, I have been visiting Japan almost every year since. I have visited to Kyoto, Okinawa, and Nikko, but mostly Tokyo.

Last year I was looking for a special birthday present for my wife and I found it in a wonderful book about Japanese *ryokan*. When I read the article about Hakkei-tei in Hikone and looked at the pictures, I decided immediately that this *ryokan* was the place to spend her birthday!

When we arrived, we were amazed by the beauty of this traditional, well-preserved *ryokan*. In fact, it is the oldest ryokan in Japan built in 1677, it was a guesthouse of the Lords of Hikone. Connected to the guesthouse (which is built over a pond) is a tea-house, surrounded by a lovely garden – a Genkyu-en. On the nearby mountain top is one of Japan's most beautiful castles!

Hakkei-tei's landlords do a great job: Not only they do restore and maintain the house, but they provide excellent cooking and service. He is the 'chef de cuisine,' while she serves the guests. Their dinner was surely one of the most exquisite culinary experiences of my life.

In Hakkei-tei, TIME both flies and stands still. When dinner is served, it is a show for your eyes and your stomach: beautiful and exquisite, dish after dish is served, every time a different look, a different way, a different taste. Two hours of never-ending gastronomic pleasure. While enjoying

Hikone
Shiga

Once upon a time there was a Lord, who lived in an wonderful castle. Whe he invited important guests, he hosted them in a seperate guest-house (genkyu-en) on the bottom of the hill. There was even a tea-house and a garden which the guests enjoyed, and when evening came they had the most beautiful view of the moon... And so it is stll today.

the dinner, time flew so fast that we did not even realize that it had become dark outside! The garden and the pond were silent, and were illuminated in a very refined way. All of a sudden, we couldn't believe our eyes: we saw trees growing downwards! Yes, really! The pond was so still, without a single wave, that the reflection made the trees look as if they were growing downwards. At that moment, we felt plunge right into a fairy tale-world, observed by the luminous fairy tale-castle on the hill. Time stood still...

The following sentence, which I read, which I read in the *ryokan* book, comes to mind: "The view, the whole atmosphere of this place is pure magic, and when you have to leave Hakkei-tei again with a heavy heart, you not only have to separate from an alien world, but you have difficulties readapting to your own world again."

So my advice would be: Don't wait for somebody's birthday to visit Hakkei-tei!

Editor's memo   Hikone: casatle town is now popular for its mascot

Situated in the central-eastern part of Shiga Prefecture, Hikone is best known for Hikone Castle and was flourished as a castle town of the Ii family. The family played an active part in the hereditary Tokugawa Shogunate in the Edo Period. Hikone lies on the Nakasendo, one of the most important trading routes during the Edo Period, and is home to two former post stations, Toriimoto-juku and Takamiya-juku.

Hikone Castle his situated near Lake Biwa and Kinki-zan Hill. Its three-layered chalk castle tower still maintains its noble and heroic appearance as a symbol of the city. It is also designated as a national treasure. Genkyu-en, the old garden of a feudal lord, is another tourist attraction.

The castle of Ishida Mitsunari, the leader who lost the Battle of Sekigahara, is located at Mount Sawa, about one kilometer east of Hikone Castle. At the foot of the mountain, there are a number of historical spots such as Ryotan-ji Temple, Ohora Bensaiten, and several temples and shrines associated with the Ii family.

In recent years, the town has become famous for its official mascot "Hik-onyan", the white samurai cat.

Mirror, mirror on the wall, who is the fairest one of all?

Magical mystery tour is waiting to take you away, waiting to take you away. (The Beatles). All photos in this article weare taken by Volker Quandt himself when he visited the town.

Zubin Mehta, India

recommends:
Cherry Blossoms

Conductor who has directed several orchestras around the world. He continues to support the discovery and furtherance of musical talents around the world.

Number of visits: many

I have visited Japan for many, many times by now! My favorite sites include:
- Hakone - with its beautiful japanese style hotel and the wonderful modern art museum
- Seto Inland Sea - with its various islands
- Nagoya - and a visit to the Toyota car manufacturing plant

And of course ,
- The peak of the Cherry Blossoms - In the 1st week of April, anywhere in Japan.

Editor's memo   Nagoya: commercial city with the history of castle town

Locating at the heart of central Japan, Nagoya developed as the castle town of the Owari, one of the three branches of the ruling Tokugawa family during the Edo Period. The region's are traditional industries include ceramics and textiles, and today's key industries such as automobiles and machine tools.

Toyota has its headquarters in Toyota city and many of its domestic production plants in the region around Nagoya. There is also the Toyota Kaikan Museum next to its headquarters.

A significant symbol of the town is the Nagoya Castle, built in 1612 and widely known for the golden dolphins adorning its rooftop. The Atsuta-jingu Shrine, the Nagoya City Art Museum, and other sites attract numerous tourists each year.

Hanami is translated literally as "flower blooming", but for the Japanese, it entails mainly the viewing of cherry blossoms. No matter the specific species of cherry trees, they are normally organized and clustered together in parks, temples, shrines, and other viewing areas. The photo above is Cherry Blossom Festival Cherry Blossom Festival in Shinjuku Gyoen, in Tokyo.

What is an onsen or a hot spring?

Onsen technically means either a place or phenomenon where hot water springs from the ground. The water must also have at least more than one of 19 compounds, including manganese, ion and radium salt, to qualify it as at spring. Often in Japan, the springs have much higher levels of such compounds than required.

Each onsen location offers different water types and qualities, but a common characteristic among them is the rich content of minerals in the water that is known to be beneficial for health. Traditionally in Japan, many who hope to cure chronic diseases often immerse themselves in therapeutic baths called "tooji", and stay for longer periods at such spas.

● Noboribetsu Onsen Hokkaido

• Take JR Muroran Line from Shin-Chitose Airport to Noboribetsu station and from the station to the hot spring area by bus.

Noboribetsu Onsen area is one of the most famous Hokkaido's resorts with 11 different types of hot springs-including such as sulfur and salt. Just above this hot spring town, there is a valley "Jigokudani," meaning hell valley which displays hot steam vents, sulfurous streams and other volcanic activity, a main source of Noboribetsu's hot spring waters as well. Scenic walking trails from the valley through the wooded hills above Noboribetsu is attractive, too. So as unique entertainment facilities such as the Date Jidaimura, a history theme park and the Noboribetsu Bear Park.

● Kinugawa Onsen Tochigi

• Take Tobu Isesaki-Nikko-Kinugawa Line from Asakusa station to Kinugawa-onsen station. And take bus from the station to Oku-Kinu-onsenkyo.

Kinugawa Onsen is a popular hot spring resort town along the Kinugawa River in Tochigi prefecture. The mildly alkaline simple springs are said to have been discovered in 1752. Today, the town is centered around the large hotels lining the riverbank, and has several public baths which are available to anybody.

● Kusatsu Onsen Gunma

• JR limited express Kusatsu, Naganohara-Kusatsu-guchi station, and take bus to Kusatsu-onsen. And transfer at Kusatsu-onsen bus terminal to Shirane-kazan.

Situating in Gunma prefecture, Kusatsu is one of the most famous hot spring resorts in Japan. It was listed as one of "Three Famed Hot Springs" by Confucian poet Hayashi Razan of the Edo Period, along with Gero in Gifu and Arima in Hyogo.

Kusatsu Onsen is known for large volumes of high quality spring water, which gushe forth throughout the town with the smell of sulfur. The town is popular particularly with women because it is said its hot spring water makes the skin beautiful. Also, in winter, a number of people visit Kusatsu to enjoy skiing or snowboarding.

● Hakone 17 Spas Kanagawa

• Take Odakyu Line to Hakone-Yumoto station. Or take JR Tokaido Line to Odawara, and to Hakone-Yumoto station by Hakone Tozan Line.

Hakone Yumoto is a historical hot springs town dating back to the Nara Period in the 8th century. There are more than 70 sources of hot-spring water around this area, where is the entrance to Hakone with a lot of various hot spring facilities, shops and restaurants. The Alkaline Pure Springs are good for neuralgia, joint pain and excessive sensitivity to cold.

● Yugawara Onsen Kanagawa

• From Tokyo station to Yugawara station by JR Tokaido Line.

Yugawara Onsen is located along the Chitose River that straddles Shizuoka and Kanagawa prefectures. Ryokan (Japanese-style inns) are found mostly at the foot of the mountains adding the tasteful charm to the peaceful hot spring site.

Thanks to a mild climate throughout the year, Yugawara is a popular health resort desitnation. The picturesque scenery has long inspired poet, writers and artists, to the extent that the hot spring appeared on Manyo-syu, the oldest anthology of tanka compiked in the eighth century.

● Atami Onsen Shizuoka/Izu

• From Tokyo station to Atami station by JR Tokaido Shinkansen Line.

Blessed with a mild climate and the beauty of nature, Atami Onsen is located at the Izu Peninsula, along the coast of the Bay of Sagami. The area flourished as the therapeutic bath site in Meiji Period (1868-1912) and is still recognized as the one of Japan's great hot spring resorts. The magnificent ocean as well as mountain views of Atami have inspired various cultural figures resulting masterpieces of Japanese literature and arts.

● Ito Onsen `Shizuoka/Izu`

• JR Tokaido Shinkansen Line, Atami station, and to Ito station by JR Ito Line.

Being one of Japan's most famous hot spring resorts, Ito Onsen boasts its abundant gushing volume with about 32,000 liters per minute. There are over hundred accommodation facilities, including ryokan (Japanese-style Inns), modern resort hotels and B&B pensions. Thanks to a mild climate and a picturesque setting close to central Tokyo, Ito Onsen enjoys many international visitors throughout the year.

● Shuzenji Onsen `Shizuoka/Izu`

• JR Tokaido Shinkansen Line, Mishima station, and to Shuzenji station by Izu-Hakone Sunzu Line.

Known as the oldest hot spring in Izu Peninsula, Shuzenji Onsen is chosen as the one of Japan's 100 great hot springs. It is situated along the Katsura River and is surrounded by mountains that showcase nature in all seasons magnificently. Along the river, there is a foot bathing place and the temple named Shuzen-ji (Shuzen Temple), the origin of the name of this area.

● Dogo Onsen `Ehime`

• From Matsuyama Airport to Dogo-onsen by bus. Or take JR Seto-ohashi/Yosan Line from Okayama station to Matsuyama station, and to Dogo-onsen station by Iyo Line.

Located in Matsuyama, Ehime prefecture, Dogo Onsen is Japan's oldest hot spring, a public bath house, dating back to more than 3000 years, having been mentioned in both the "Manyo-shu" and "Nihon-shoki" (the first and second oldest books in Japanese history, respectively). Dogo Onsen has many relations to great writers. It was the favorite retreat of a renowned novelist Natsume Soseki when he was working near Matsuyama as a teacher. In Soseki's loosely autobiographical novel "Botchan," the eponymous main character is a frequent visitor to the onsen, the only place he says he likes in the area.

● Beppu Onsen `Kanagawa`

• Take JR Nippo Honsen Line from Oita station to Beppu station.

Beppu, locating on the coast of Beppu bay in Oita prefecture, is one of the Japan's best popular hot spring resorts with over 3,000 thermal springs, believed it ranks first in gush volume in the country, as well as in a high place in the world in the variety of chemical ingredients. The Beppu Onsen spa resort consists of eight hot spring areas, including Beppu, Hamawaki, Horita, Myoban and Kannawa, which are collectively called "Beppu Hatto." The most favored attraction in this area is touring the boiling "Hells of Beppu," which six of hells are located in the

● Yufuin Onsen `Oita`

- Take JR Main Kyudai Line from Oita station to Yufuin station.

Yufuin Onsen resort area has been constantly ranked as the most favorite onsen resort in Kyusyu among travelers. It is a very quiet and relaxed spa town located in a valley basin beneath the Mt. Yufu-dake, which is the landmark of the town. Despite becoming a famous hot-spring resort, the rural landscape remains unchanged, and it gives visitors tranquility and peace of mind. It is one of only a few resorts in Kyushu that harmonizes well a simple mountain village with modern tourist facilities.

● Kurokawa Onsen `Kumamoto`

- Take JR Yufu-DXExpress to Bungo-Nakamura station, and from Bungo-Nakamura to Iida-kogen-kyoku-mae (Kuju) by Nishitetsu highway bus. Or take Nishitetsu highway bus from Tenjin Bus Center to Kurokawa-onsen.

Kurokawa Onsen area is located in Minamiogunicho, Kumamoto prefecture. Almost all Japanese-style inns have open-air spas. In the office and information center of the hotel association, "Onsen tegata," a ticket made of cedars (1200 yen), is available to chose three hot-spring inns to bathe.

● Asama Onsen `Nagano`

- Take JR Chuo Line (limited express) to Matsumoto station, and from the station to Asama-Onsen by bus.

The Asama-onsen is one of the most popular hot springs in Nagano. It is said to be effective for curing rheumatic diseases, gastronomical troubles and external wounds. In the olden days, only the feudal lords residing in Matsumoto Castle were entitled to use this hot spring. Today it is the gateway to the scenic sites in central Nagano such as the Northern Japan Alps.

● Jigokudani Onsen/Snow Monkey Park `Nagano`

- Nagano Dentetsu Line, Yudanaka sta., take bus Uebayashi Onsen stop, and a 30 min walk from the stop. To Snow Monkey Park, take a Dentetsu bus to Shibu Onsen Wagobashi stop, or take shuttle bus from Yudanaka sta.

Located in the small valley of Yokoyu River, Jigokudani Snow Monkey Park has attracted many people since its foundation in 1964. It is called Jigokudani or hell valley because of its steep cliffs and bubbling hot springs invokes an image of the hell. For monkey, however, it is a paradise and you can observe the lives of Japanese macaques close by, and during the winter time, you can see them dipping in the hot springs in deep snow. The hot spring itself is open for people to enjoy bathing in the beautiful scenery for all seasons.

● Waketokuyama `Japanese Cuisine`

- 5-1-5 Minami-Azabu, Minato-ku, Tokyo • **TEL** (+81) 3-5789-3838 • **OPEN** 5pm-11pm (L.O. 9pm) • **CLOSED** Sundays • VISA / JCB / DINERS / AMEX / MASTER • 15,750-20,000 yen

Authentic Japanese kaiseki with omakase (fixed) course which changes every two weeks using the season's best ingredients. Awarded 2 stars by Michelin Guide Tokyo. Reservation strongly recommended.

● Ishikawa `Japanese Cuisine`

- 1F Takamura Bldg., 5-37 Kagurazaka, Shinjuku-ku, Tokyo • **TEL** (+81) 3-5225-0173 • http://kagurazaka-ishikawa.co.jp • **OPEN** 5:30pm-midnight • **CLOSED** Sundays and public holidays • VISA / MASTER / JCB • 15,000 / 19,000 yen

Authentic Japanese kaiseki with 2 omakase courses and special "snow crab" course in winter. Reservation strongly recommended. Awarded 3 stars by Michelin Guide Tokyo.

● Tora kuma mogura `Japanese Cuisine`

- B1F LaPole Azabu-Juban, 2-12-7 Azabu-Juban, Minato-ku, Tokyo • **TEL** (+81) 3-5441-2511 • http://www.kumamogura.jp • **OPEN** 6pm-2:30am (L.O.) [Sat / public holidays] 6pm-11pm (L.O.) • **CLOSED** Sundays and Monday (if Mon falls on a public holiday) • VISA / MASTER / JCB / AMEX / DINERS • 8,000-10,000 yen

Seafood restaurant in prime Azabu-Juban. Its specialties including fish and horse sashimi. Prices are not indicated in the menu list, so inquire before ordering.

● Ayumasa `Japanese Cuisine`

- 4-21-14 Shinbashi, Minato-ku, Tokyo • **TEL** (+81) 3-3431-7448 • http://ayumasa.main.jp • **OPEN** 5pm-10pm, [Sat] 5pm-9pm • **CLOSED** Sun, public holidays and the 2nd and 4th Saturdays of the months (Nov-May) • VISA / MASTER / DINERS / AMEX • 15,000 yen ~

Sweetfish (ayu) specialties and authentic Japanese dishes. Courses and a la carte available. Awarded 1 star by Michelin Guide Tokyo.

● Kanda `Japanese Cuisine`

- 1F Calm Motoazabu, 3-6-34 Motoazabu, Minato-ku, Tokyo • **TEL** (+81) 3-5786-0150 • **OPEN** 6pm-10pm (L.O.) • **CLOSED** Sundays and public holidays • VISA / MASTER / JCB / AMEX / DINERS • 20,000 yen ~

Authentic Japanese kaiseki with omakase course by a French-speaking owner chef. Known for tasty conger (anago) sushi. Awarded 3 stars by Michelin Guide Tokyo.

● Ginza Kojyu `Japanese Cuisine`

- 1F The Second Sanyu Bldg. 8-5-25 Ginza, Chuo-ku, Tokyo • **TEL** (+81) 3-6215-9544
- http://www.kojyu.jp • **OPEN** [Mon-Fri] 5:30pm-11pm (L.O.) [Sat] 5:30pm-9:30pm (L.O.)
- **CLOSED** Sundays and public holidays • VISA / JCB / MASTER / AMEX / DINERS
- 13,650 / 21,000 / 26,250 yen

Authentic Japanese kaiseki with 3 courses. Good selection of sake and French wine to go with the dishes. Reservation recommended. Awarded 3 stars by Michelin Guide Tokyo.

● Kyubey `Sushi`

- 8-7-6 Ginza, Chuo-ku, Tokyo • **TEL** (+81) 3-3571-6523 • http://www.kyubey.jp
- **OPEN** [Lunch] 11:30am-2pm [Dinner] 5pm-10pm • **CLOSED** Sundays, public holidays, Obon and Year-end / New Year holidays • VISA / MASTER / AMEX / DINERS / JCB
- Lunch: 8,400 yen ~ / Dinner: 15,750 yen ~

One of the representative sushi restaurants in prestigious Ginza. Reasonable menus are available at lunch but expect large crowdsare available at lunch but expect large crowds.

● Sushisho `Sushi`

- 1F Yorindo Bldg. 1-11 Yotsuya, Shinjuku-ku Tokyo • **TEL** (+81) 3-3351-6387 • **OPEN** [Lunch] 11:30am until sold-out [Dinner] 6pm-10:30pm • **CLOSED** Sundays and Monday (if Mon falls on apublic holiday) • JCB / AMEX / VISA • Lunch: 1,000-2,000 yen / Dinner: 20,000 yen ~

Known for colorful bara-chirashi sushi (sushi bowl with various ingredients). Traditional sushi and Japanese-style finger foods are also available at night.

● Kozasa Sushi `Sushi`

- 1F The Second Ginza Karera Bldg., 8-6-18 Ginza, Chuo-ku, Tokyo • **TEL** (+81) 3-3289-2227 • **OPEN** [Lunch] noon-2pm [Dinner] 5:30pm-10pm • **CLOSED** Sundays and public holidays • JCB / AMEX / VISA / MASTER / DINERS • Lunch: 10,000-15,000 yen / Dinner: 20,000 yen ~

Authentic Edomae (old Tokyo) style sushi, known for its rich taste with ingredients often simmered in broth or immersed in soy source.

● Sushi no Midori Souhonten `Sushi`

- 1-20-7 Umegaoka, Setagaya-ku, Tokyo • **TEL** (+81) 3-3429-1166 • http://www.sushinomidori.co.jp • **OPEN** 11am-9:45pm (L.O.) [Sundays and public holidays] -8:45pm (L.O.) • **CLOSED** Open Daily • VISA / MASTER / JCB • 3,000-4,000 yen

Reasonable, high-quality sushi chain famous for sushi using whole conger (anago). 7 outlets in Tokyo including Ginza, Shibuya and Akasaka.

● Roppongi Fukuzushi [Sushi]

- 5-7-8 Roppongi, Minato-ku, Tokyo • **TEL** (+81) 3-3402-4116 • http://www.roppongifukuzushi.com • **OPEN** [Lunch] 11:30am-1:30pm (L.W.) [Dinner] 5:30pm-10pm (L.W.)
- **CLOSED** Sundays and public holidays • VISA / MASTER / JCB / AMEX / DINERS
- Lunch: 2,625 yen / Dinner: 6,300 yen

One of the old sushi restaurants in Tokyo established in 1917 that also serves authentic Japanese foods. Bar lounge inside. English speaking staff available.

● Sushi Mizutani [Sushi]

- 9F JUNO Bldg., 8-7-7 Ginza, Chuo-ku, Tokyo • **TEL** (+81) 3-3573-5258 • **OPEN** [Lunch] 11:30am-1:30pm [Dinner] 5pm-9:30pm • **CLOSED** Sundays and public holidays • Lunch: 18,000 yen / Dinner: 18,000 yen

Edomae sushi restaurant with omakase and additional ala carte, run by the owner chef trained at Michelin 3-star Sukiyabashi Jiro. Awarded 3 stars by Michelin Guide Tokyo.

● Rakutei [Tempura]

- Music In Akasaka, 6-8-1 Akasaka, Minato-ku, Tokyo • **TEL** (+81) 3-3585-3743
- **OPEN** [Lunch] enter by noon [Dinner] 5pm-8:30pm • **CLOSED** Mondays • 15,000 yen • Advanced reservations required.

Tempura with various vegetables and seafood, cooked using only fresh white sesame seed oil. Reservation strongly recommended since there are only 10 seats. Awarded 2 stars by Michelin Guide.

● Kondo [Tempura]

- 9F Sakaguchi Bldg., 5-5-13 Ginza, Chuo-ku, Tokyo • **TEL** (+81) 3-5568-0923
- **OPEN** [Lunch] noon-1:30pm, 1:30pm-3pm [Dinner] 5pm-8:30pm (L.O.) • **CLOSED** Sundays and Monday (If Mon falls on apublic holiday) • VISA / MASTER / JCB / AMEX / DINERS • Lunch: 6,300 yen / Dinner: 10,500 yen ~ • Other outlet is in Roppongi.

Tempura restaurant in historical art deco Yamanoue Hotel (Hilltop Hotel) loved by famous Japanese writers such as Mishima Yukio and Ikenami Shotaro.

● Yamanoue [Tempura]

- 1-1 Kanda-Surugadai, Chiyoda-ku, Tokyo • **TEL** (+81) 3-3293-2831 • http://www.yamanoue-hotel.co.jp • **OPEN** [Breakfast] 7am-10:30am [Lunch] 11am-3pm [Dinner] 5pm-9pm, [weekends, PH] 3pm-9pm • **CLOSED** Open Daily • JCB / VISA / MASTER / AMEX / DINERS • Breakfast: 2,451 yen / Lunch: 6,000 yen ~ / Dinner: 15,000 yen ~

Tempura restaurant in historical art deco Yamanoue Hotel (Hilltop Hotel) loved by famous Japanese writers such as Mishima Yukio and Ikenami Shotaro. Other outlet in Roppongi area.

● Mikawa [Tempura]

- 3-4-7 Nihonbashi-Kayabacho, Chuo-ku, Tokyo • **TEL** (+81) 3-3664-9843 • **OPEN** [Lunch] 11:30am-1:30pm [Dinner] 5pm-9:30pm • **CLOSED** Wed • VISA / MASTER / JCB / AMEX / DINERS • Lunch: 1,200-3,000 yen / Dinner: 10,000-15,000 yen

One of the well-known tempura and ten-don (tempura rice bowl) restaurants in Tokyo's financial Kayabacho area. Offers reasonable lunch but expect for a long queue. Other outlet in Roppongi area. Awarded 1 star by Michelin Guide Tokyo.

● Tsurutontan [Soba/Udon]

- 3-14-12 Roppongi, Minato-ku, Tokyo • **TEL** (+81) 3-5786-2626 • http://www.tsuru-tontan.co.jp • **OPEN** 11am-8am (on next day) • **CLOSED** Open Daily • VISA / JCB / AMEX / DINERS • 1,000-5,000 yen

Fashonable udon noodle restaurant using fresh house made noodles served with hot or cold soup. 10 outlets in Tokyo and Kansai area including Roppongi and Haneda Airport.

● Mimiu [Soba/Udon]

- 4F Shibuya Mark City West, 1-12-5 Dogenzaka, Shibuya-ku, Tokyo • **TEL** (+81) 3-5459-2620 • http://www.mimiu.co.jp • **OPEN** [Lunch] 11am-3pm (L.O.) [Dinner] 5pm-9:30pm (L.O.) [Weekends, public holidays] 11am-9:30pm (L.O.) • **CLOSED** Open Daily • VISA / DINERS / AMEX / JCB • 3,000-5,000 yen

Famous for its "udon-suki," a hot pot with various ingredients and udon noodle. Also offers shabu-shabu and kaiseki dishes. 22 outlets in Kanto, Kansai and Chubu regions.

● Nodaiwa [Unagi]

- 1-5-4 Higashi-Azabu, Minato-ku, Tokyo • **TEL** (+81) 3-3583-7852 • http://www.nodaiwa.co.jp • **OPEN** [Lunch] 11am-1:30pm (L.O.) [Dinner] 5pm-8pm (L.O.) • **CLOSED** Sundays and the day of the ox in summer • VISA / MASTER / DINERS • Lunch: 3,000 yen ~ / Dinner: 8,000 yen ~

Established 160 years ago, this restaurant specializes in eel (unagi) dishes. Menu includes baked, teriyaki and don (rice bowl) style. Awarded 1 star by Michelin Guide Tokyo.

● Ishibashi [Unagi]

- 2-4-29 Suido, Bunkyo-ku, Tokyo • **TEL** (+81) 3-3813-8038 • http://unagi-ishibashi.com • **OPEN** [Lunch]11:30am-1:30pm (L.O.) [Dinner] 6pm-7:30pm (L.O.) • **CLOSED** Sundays, Mondays, public holidays and the day of the ox in summer • Lunch: 2,700 yen ~ / Dinner: 11,000 yen ~

100 year-old unagi restaurant offers unajyu (unagi over rice) in 3 different prices. Be patient after ordering for the unagi to be cooked. Awarded 1 star by Michelin Guide.

● Ochaya Wadaya Ginza `Shabu Shabu`

- 6-6-11 Ginza, Chuo-ku, Tokyo • TEL (+81) 3-3569-0410 • http://www.wada-ya.com
- OPEN 5pm-10pm (L.O.) • CLOSED Sundays • VISA / MASTER / JCB / AMEX
- 6,500 yen • For reservation details check the website.

Known for light-seasoned Kansai-style pork *shabu shabu*, or Japanese hot pot. Pork can be chosen from four brands produced in different areas. Unique lights are decorated by autographs of Japanese celebrities as it is run by the famous celebrity singer Akiko Wada.

● Butagumi `Tonkatsu`

- 2-24-9 Nishi-Azabu, Minato-ku, Tokyo • TEL (+81) 3-5466-6775 • http://www.butagumi.com • OPEN [Lunch] 11:30am-2pm (L.O.) [Dinner] 6pm-10pm (L.O.)
- CLOSED Mondays and Tuesday (if Monday falls on apublic holiday) • VISA / MASTER / JCB / AMEX / DINERS • 4,000 yen

The restaurant is run by a French chef-turned tonkatsu chef. It offers only pork cutlet from various brands, such as Iberico, Okinawa, Yonezawa, Hungarian, etc.

● Maisen `Tonkatsu`

- 4-8-5 Jingu-mae, Shibuya-ku, Tokyo • TEL Free dial within Japan 0120-428-485
- http://mai-sen.com • OPEN 11am-10pm (L.O.) • CLOSED Open Daily • VISA / MASTER / JCB / AMEX / DINERS • 3,000 yen

The chain restaurant with 6 outlets specializes in Japanese Berkshire pork cutlet (tonkatsu). It also offers fried prawns and course dishes.

● Tonki `Tonkatsu`

- 1-1-2 Shimo-Meguro, Meguro-ku, Tokyo • TEL (+81) 3491-9928 • OPEN 4pm-10:45pm (L.O.) • CLOSED Tuesdays and third Monday of the month • VISA / MASTER / JCB / AMEX • 2,000 yen ~

One of the popular tonkatsu places in Meguro that offers Japan-bred pork fried with pure lard. Known for its katsudon with a lightly cooked egg over it.

● Tora `Izakaya`

- 3-49-1 Ebisu, Shibuya-ku, Tokyo • TEL (+81) 3-3440-0917 • http://www.tola.co.jp
- OPEN [Lunch] 11:30am-2pm [Dinner] 6pm-midnight (L.O.) • CLOSED Sundays
- VISA / MASTER / JCB / AMEX / DINERS • Lunch: 1,000 yen / Dinner: 6,000 yen~

Japanese restaurant known for its charcoal grilling of seafood and meats. It also serves ochazuke (rice in tea-based broth) with various toppings, such as tempura and sashimi.

● Shin Hinomoto Andy's `Izakaya`

• 2-4-4 Yurakucho, Chiyoda-ku, Tokyo • **TEL** (+81) 3-3214-8021 • **OPEN** 5pm-11:30pm (L.O.) • **CLOSED** Sandays • 3,000-5,000 yen

Old style izakaya underneath the elevated JR railway tracks. Various pub menus using fresh seafood and vegetables with reasonable pricing; menu includes sashimi and tempura. Smoking allowed.

● Tachimichi-ya `Izakaya`

• B1F 30-8 Sarugakucho, Shibuya-ku, Tokyo • **TEL** (+81) 3-5459-3431 • **OPEN** 6pm-4am [Sat, Sun and public holidays] -midnight • **CLOSED** Open Daily • 3,000-4,000 yen

Izakaya in trendy Daikanyama where many young Japanese celebrities regularly visit. Modern Izakaya dishes with seafood, meat and vegetables. Homemade ramen with chicken broth is one of their specialties.

● Bar Rouge `Bar`

• B1 FS Bldg., 3-20-6 Shinjuku, Shinjuku-ku, Tokyo • **TEL** (+81) 3-3354-7688
• http://hwsa5.gyao.ne.jp/bar-rouge/ • **OPEN** 6pm-3:30am (L.O.) [Sundays] -midnight
• **CLOSED** Open Daily • VISA / MASTER / DINERS / AMEX / JCB • 4,500 yen

Located near bustle nightclub district Kabukicho, Bar Rouge provides quiet ambiance with a chic black and red interior. Various liquors and cocktails served in Baccarat glasses by veteran bartenders.

● Sazanka `Teppanyaki`

• 11F Hotel Okura, 2-10-4 Toranomon, Minato-ku, Tokyo • **TEL** (+81) 3-3505-6071
• http://www.hotelokura.co.jp • **OPEN** [Lunch] 11:30am-2:30pm [Dinner] 5:30pm-9:30pm • **CLOSED** Open Daily • VISA / MASTER / JCB / AMEX / DINERS • Lunch: 8,000-10,000 yen / Dinner: 20,000-30,000 yen

Teppanyaki restaurant in prestigious Hotel Okura. The chef cooks prawns, vegetables, meats and rice on hot plate in front of you. Famous for its sirloin steak and selection of wine.

● Shima `Steak`

• B1 Nihonbashi MM Bld, 3-5-12 Nihonbashi, Cyuo-ku, Tokyo • **TEL** (+81)3-3271-7889 • **OPEN** [Lunch] noon-1pm [Dinner] 6pm-9pm • **CLOSED** Sandays • VISA / MASTER / JCB / AMEX / DINERS • Lunch: 15,000 yen / Dinner: 30,000 yen

Western-style steak house with open kitchen offers course menu and a la carte. Size of steak can be ordered from 150g. Also famous for its crab cream croquette.

● Motsuyaki Inagaki Barbecue

- 3-25-4 Higashi-Komagata, Sumida-ku, Tokyo • **TEL** (+81) 3-3623-6389 • **OPEN** 5pm-11:30pm (L.O.) • **CLOSED** Selected days • 2,000-3,000 yen

Popular izakaya serving cheap Japanese pub snacks such as motsu-yaki (roast pork giblets) and motsu-nikomi (stewed pork giblets). Wide variety of izakaya-style foods and kid-friendly dishes such as hamburger steak.

● Teppo Kurume Hanabatake Yakitori

- 921-15 Nishi-machi, Kurume-shi, Fukuoka • **TEL** (+81) 942-39-7139 • http://www.teppo.jp • **OPEN** 5pm-0:30am (L.O.) • **CLOSED** Open Daily • VISA / JCB • 5,000 yen

Kurume-style yakitori (grilled chicken on sticks) known for its various ingredients including pork, beef (especially giblets), seafood and vegetables. 4 outlets in Kurume, the third largest city in Fukuoka.

● Kinryusan Barbecue

- 1F Daiichi Mansion, 3-14-1 Shirokane, Minato-ku, Tokyo • **TEL** (+81) 3-3446-8156 • **OPEN** 6pm-9:15pm (L.O.) • **CLOSED** Mondays • 8,000 yen • Reservations required

Korean style BBQ restaurant awarded the Hall of Fame by the Japanese BBQ gourmet website. Known for its top-quality loin with original garlic source.

● Ginza Lion Beer Hall

- 7-9-20 Ginza, Chuo-ku, Tokyo • **TEL** (+81) 3-3571-2590 • http://www.ginzalion.jp • **OPEN** 11:30am-11pm, [Sundays, public holidays] -10:30pm • **CLOSED** Open Daily • VISA / MASTER / DINERS / AMEX / JCB • 3,000 yen

Long-established beer restaurant chain in Japan since 1899 operated by Sapporo, a major beer manufacturer. Enjoy draft beer and its signature roasted beef at the oldest Ginza outlet, decorated with mosaic walls.

● Montoak Café Restaurant

- 6-1-9 Jingumae, Shibuya-ku, Tokyo • **TEL** (+81) 3-5468-5928 • http://www.montoak.com • **OPEN** 11am-2:30am (L.O.) • **CLOSED** Open Daily • VISA / MASTER / DINERS / AMEX / JCB • 1,000-4,000 yen

Western-style café and bar with spacious terrace seats that opens daily until 3 am. Serves light meals and sweets as well as variety of drinks from coffee to cocktails. Kids and pets welcome.

● New York Grill `American`

- Park Hyatt Tokyo, 3-7-1-2 Nishi-Shinjuku, Shinjuku-ku, Tokyo • **TEL** (+81) 3-5323-3458 • http://www.tokyo.park.hyatt.com • **OPEN** [Lunch]11:30am-2:30pm [Dinner] 5:30pm-9:30pm • **CLOSED** Open Daily • VISA / MASTER / DINERS / AMEX / JCB • Lunch: 7,000 yen / Dinner: 30,000 yen

American-style dining on the 52nd floor overlooking skyscrapers of Shinjuku. Known for its premium Japanese beef selection, grilled specialties and breathtaking views.

● Monna Lisa `French`

- Marunouchi Bld, 2-4-1 Marunouchi, Chiyoda-ku, Tokyo • **TEL** (+81) 3-3240-5775 • http://www.monnalisa.co.jp • **OPEN** [Lunch] 11:30am-2pm (L.O.) [Dinner] 5:30pm-9:30pm (L.O.) [Sat / Sun] 5:30pm-9pm (L.O.) • VISA / MASTER / DINERS / AMEX / JCB • Lunch: 3,750 yen ~ / Dinner: 6,800 yen ~

French cuisine served by a chef trained at the prestigious Guy Savoy. Located on the top of Marunouchi Bldg, with another outlet in Ebisu. Awarded 1 star by Michelin Guide.

● Joël Robuchon `French`

- Ebisu Garden Place, 1-13-1 Mita, Meguro-ku, Tokyo • **TEL** (+81) 3-5424-1347 • http://www.robuchon.jp • **OPEN** [Lunch] 11:30am-2pm (L.O.) [Sat / Sun / public holidays] noon-2pm (L.O.) [Dinner] 6pm-9:30pm (L.O.) • **CLOSED** Fixed holiday • VISA / MASTER / JCB / AMEX • Lunch: 8,000 yen ~ / Dinner: 22,500 yen ~

Its castle-like Ebisu main outlet consists of casual dining and fine French dining by the celebrity chef Joel Robuchon. Awarded 3 stars by Michelin Guide Tokyo.

● á nu, retrouvez-vouz `French`

- 1F SR Hiroo Bld, 5-19-4 Hiroo, Shibuya-ku, Tokyo • **TEL** (+81) 3-5422-8851 • http://www.restaurant-anu.com • **OPEN** [Lunch] 11:30am-1:30pm (L.O.) [Dinner] 6pm-9pm (L.O.) • **CLOSED** Tuesdays • VISA / AMEX / DINERS • Lunch: 4,000 yen ~ / Dinner: 8,500 yen ~

French restaurant run by a young French-trained chef. Two sommeliers pair dishes with wine from 400 available options. Awarded 1 star by Michelin Guide Tokyo.

● Grand Maison Apicius `French`

- B1 Sanshi Kaikan, 1-9-4 Yuraku-cho, Chiyoda-ku, Tokyo • **TEL** (+81) 3-3214-1361 • http://www.apicius.co.jp • **OPEN** [Lunch] 11:30am-2pm (L.O.) [Dinner] 5:30pm-9pm (L.O.) • **CLOSED** Sundays • VISA / MASTER / JCB / AMEX / DINERS • Lunch: 10,000 yen / Dinner: 25,000 yen

Prestigious grand maison in Japan serving since 1983. Located in Marunouchi area near Imperial Palace. Authentic French served in Japanese bone china. Upscale ambience.

● Chez Inno `French`

- 1F Meiji Kyobashi Bld, 2-4-16 Kyobashi, Cyuou-ku, Tokyo • **TEL** (+81) 3-3274-2020
- http://www.chezinno.jp • **OPEN** [Lunch] 11:30am-2pm (L.O.) [Dinner] 6pm-9pm
(L.O.) • **CLOSED** Sundays • VISA / MASTER / JCB / AMEX / DINERS • Lunch: 3,780
/ 4,830 / 6,300 / 8,400 yen / Dinner: 13,650 / 15,750 / 21,000 yen

French restaurant run by the celebrity chef Inoue Noboru, trained at Michel Troisgros and Maxim's de Paris. More than 10,000 wine options served by a veteran sommelier.

● Quintessence `French`

- 1F Barbizon 25, 5-4-7 Shirokanedai, Minato-ku, Tokyo • **TEL** (+81) 3-5791-3711
(except reservation) • http://www.quintessence.jp • **OPEN** [Lunch] noon-1pm (L.O.)
[Dinner] 6:30pm-8:30pm (L.O.) • **CLOSED** unfixed holiday • Lunch: 12,000 yen /
Dinner: 30,000 yen • For reservation details check the website.

Contemporary French served only by "menu carte blanche" (chef's selected menu) which changes daily based on fresh seasonal products. Awarded 3 stars by Michelin Guide TKY.

● Cuisine[s] Michel Troisgros `French`

- 1F Hyatt Regency Tokyo, 2-7-2 Nishi-Shinjuku, Shinjuku-ku, Tokyo • **TEL** (+81) 3-3348-
1234 • http://www.troisgros.jp • **OPEN** [Lunch] 11:30am-1:30pm (L.W.) [Dinner] 6pm-
8:30pm (L.W.) • **CLOSED** Wed (Jan-Nov) • Lunch: 8,000 yen / Dinner: 20,000 yen

The only restaurant outside France named after this celebrity owner chef. French dishes made by various ingredients from Japan, France and the Mediterranean. Awarded 2 stars by Michelin Guide Tokyo.

● Le Manoir D'hastings `French`

- B1 MST Bld, 6-5-1 Ginza, Cyuou-ku, Tokyo • **TEL** (+81) 3-5568-7121 • http://
www.le-manoir-dhastings.com • **OPEN** [Lunch] 11:30am-2pm (L.W.) [Dinner] 6pm-
9pm (L.O.) • **CLOSED** Open Daily • VISA / DINERS / AMEX / JCB • Lunch: 5,000
yen / Dinner: 10,000 yen

French fusion restaurant in Ginza. Ingredients include traditional Japanese options such as soft-shell turtles and eel. Famous for its signature "Carrot Mousse."

● Chez Matsuo Shoto `French`

- 1-23-15 Shoto, Shibuya-ku, Tokyo • **TEL** (+81) 3-3485-0566 • http://www.chez-
matsuo.co.jp • **OPEN** [Lunch] noon-1pm (L.O.) [Dinner] 6pm-10:30pm (L.O.) • VISA /
MASTER / AMEX / JCB / DINERS • Lunch: 8,400 yen / Dinner: 16,800 yen~

Classic French dining in the old bungalow near Shibuya, known as the restaurant used by Prince Naruhito and Princess Masako. Spacious courtyard for aperitif and after-meal drinks. Fixed course only. Awarded 1 star by Michelin Guide Tokyo.

⊙ La Bettola da Ochlal [Italian]

• 1-21-2 Ginza, Chuou-ku, Tokyo • TEL (+81) 3-3567-5656 • http://www.la-bettola.co.jp • OPEN [Lunch] 11:30am-2pm (L.O.) [Dinner] 6:30pm-10pm (L.O), Sat. Public holiday 6pm-9:30pm • CLOSED Sun, the 1st and 3rd Mondays of the month • VISA / MASTER / JCB / AMEX / DINERS • Lunch: 2,000 yen / Dinner: 3,990 yen

Japanese celebrity chef offers classic and reasonable Italian course dishes. One of the most difficult Italian restaurants to make a reservation, so call early.

⊙ AW kitchen [Italian]

• 5F Shin Marunouchi Bld, 1-5-1 Marunouchi, Chiyoda-ku, Tokyo • TEL (+81) 3-5224-8071 • http://www.awkitchen.com • OPEN [Lunch] 11am-2:30pm [Sat / Sun / PH] -3pm (L.O.) [Dinner] 5pm-10pm [Fri] -1am [Sun / PH] -9pm (L.O.) • CLOSED unfixed holiday • VISA / MASTER / DINERS / AMEX • Lunch: 3,000 yen / Dinner: 8,000 yen

Casual Italian dining in Marunouchi. Known for its organic vegetable dishes using ingredients from selected farmers, including signature bagna càuda. 8 outlets in Tokyo and suburbs.

⊙ Ristorante Aromafresca [Italian]

• 12F Ginza Trecious, 2-6-5 Ginza, Chuo-ku, Tokyo • TEL (+81) 3-3535-6667 • http://www.aromafresca.com • OPEN 5:30pm-8:30pm (L.O.) • CLOSED Sun, the 1st Monday of the month • VISA / MASTER / DINERS / AMEX / JCB • 16,000 yen ~

One of the representative Italian restaurants in Japan. Known for its fusion with Japanese ingredients. Offered in two course meals. Also runs casual dining and café outlets in Tokyo area. Awarded 1 star by Michelin Guide Tokyo.

⊙ Ristorante Hamasaki [Italian]

• Sunlite Hill Aoyama, 4-11-13 Minami-Aoyama, Minato-ku, Tokyo • TEL (+81) 3-5772-8520 • OPEN [Lunch] Thus-Sat noon-2pm (L.O.) [Dinner] 6pm-9:30pm (L.O.) • CLOSED Sundays • VISA / MASTER / JCB / AMEX / DINERS • Lunch: 6,000-8,000 yen / Dinner: 15,000-20,000 yen

A cottage-turned Italian restaurant run by a celebrity chef trained in Italy. Various fresh Japanese ingredients used in dishes. Located in a quiet residential area in Omotesando.

⊙ Savoy [Pizzeria]

• 201 Nakaoka Bldg., 3-10-1 Motoazabu, Minato-ku, Tokyo • TEL (+81) 3-5770-7899 • http://www.savoy.vc/ • OPEN [Lunch] 11:30am-2:30pm (L.O.) [Dinner] 6pm-10pm (L.O.) • VISA / MASTER / JCB / AMEX / DINERS • Lunch: 1,000 yen / Dinner: 2,500 yen

Casual Napolitano pizza house. There are counter seats surrounding the open kitchen to view pizza to be served right from the oven.

● Nezu Museum [Tokyo]

• 6-5-1 Minami-Aoyama, Minato-ku, Tokyo • **Tel** (+81) 3-3400-2536 • Adults: 1,000 yen, College and High school: 800 yen • **OPEN** 10am-5pm • **CLOSED** Mondays and Year-end/New Year holidays • http://www.nezu-muse.or.jp • Museum shop, garden

Established in 1941 by the will of the industrialist Nezu Kaichiro, Sr., Nezu Museum holds a collection of more than 7,000 pieces of Japanese and other Asian pre-modern art, including Japanese national treasure "Irises" by Ogata Korin.

● Tokyo National Museum [Tokyo]

• 13-9 Ueno Koen, Taito-ku, Tokyo • **Tel** (+81) 3-5405-8686 • Adults: 600 yen, College: 400 yen • **OPEN** 9:30am-5pm, [Fri] -8pm, [Sat and Sun]-6pm • **CLOSED** Mondays, Year-end/New Year holidays • http://www.tnm.jp • Museum shop, restaurant

Established in 1871 as the country's first national museum, Tokyo National Museum houses and displays a comprehensive collection of art works and antiquities from Japan and other Asian countries.

● The National Museum of Western Art [Tokyo]

• 7-7 Ueno Koen, Daito-ku, Tokyo • **Tel** (+81) 3-5777-8600 • Adults: 420 yen, College: 130 yen • **OPEN** 9:30am-5pm • **CLOSED** Mondays, unfixed holiday • http://www. nmwa.go.jp • Restaurant, Museum shop

It is the only national museum dedicated to western art, inaugurated in 1959 to bring Western art closer to people. Its collection includes sculptures of Rodin and impressionist paintings. The main building is by Le Corbusier.

● Shitamachi Museum [Tokyo]

• 2-1 Ueno Koen, Daito-ku, Tokyo • **Tel** (+81) 3-3823-7451 • Adults: 300 yen, Elementary/ Jr. High/High school: 100yen • **OPEN** 9:30am-4:30pm • **CLOSED** Mon, 29th Dec-1st Jan. Unfixed holiday • http://www.taitocity.net/taito/shitamachi/index.html • In Ueno Park

The museum was established to teach the culture of the shitamachi, the area where common people lived in the Edo period. Such culture and scenery has been gradually lost after the 1923 earthquake, World War II, and the 1964 Summer Tokyo Olympics.

● Museum of Contemporary Art Tokyo [Tokyo]

• 4-1-1 Miyoshi, Koto-ku, Tokyo • **Tel** (+81) 3-5245-4111 • Adults: 500 yen, College: 400 yen • **OPEN** 10am-6pm • **CLOSED** Mondays, Year-end/New Year holidays and selected days • http://www.mot-art-museum.jp • Museum shop, restaurant, café, library

The museum holds over 4,000 contemporary art works and 100,000 books from around the world. Its restaurant with bakery and edible plants garden offers organic fusion foods.

● Hara Museum of Contemporary Art [Tokyo]

• 4-7-25 Kitashinagawa, Shinagawa-ku, Tokyo • **Tel** (+81) 3-3445-0651 • Adults: 1,000 yen, College/high school: 700 yen • **OPEN** [Tue-Fri] 11am-5pm, [Wed] 11am-8pm • http://www.haramuseum.or.jp • Online shop and museum in the website

The museum is dedicated to contemporary arts by artists based in Asia, the Americas, and Europe, spanning the entire range of post-1950 art movements. Its Bauhaus-inspired structure is a rare example of early Showa architecture.

● The National Museum of Modern Art, Tokyo [Tokyo]

• 1 Kitanomaru-koen, Chiyoda-ku, Tokyo • **Tel** (+81) 3-5777-8600 • Adults: 420 yen, College: 130 yen • **OPEN** 10am-5pm, [Fri] 10am- 8pm • **CLOSED** Mondays and Year-end/New Year holidays • http://www.momat.go.jp • Museum shop, restaurant, café

Established in 1952 by the Ministry of Education, the museum exhibits pieces of contemporary Japanese art by many important artists such as Taro Okamoto. The facility includes Gallery and a separate National Film Center (3-7-6 Kyobashi, Chuo-ku).

● Ukiyo-e Ota Memorial Museum of Art [Tokyo]

• 1-10-10 Jingu-mae, Shibuya-ku, Tokyo • **Tel** (+81) 3-3470-0880 • Adults: 700 yen, College/high school: 500 yen • **OPEN** 10:30am-5:30pm • **CLOSED** Mondays and Year-end/New Year holidays • http://www.ukiyoe-ota-muse.jp • The facility does not have elevators and slopes

This collection features more than 12,000 pieces of ukiyo-e purchased back from the West and impeccably preserved by Seizo Ota V.

● Yamatane Museum of Art [Tokyo]

• 3-12-36 Hiroo, Shibuya-ku, Tokyo • **Tel** (+81) 3-5777-8600 • Adults: 1,000 yen, College/high school: 800 yen • **OPEN** 10am-5pm • **CLOSED** Mondays and Year-end/Year Year holidays • http://www.yamatane-museum.jp

The museum holds a collection of over 1,800 works, Including rare Japanese paintings awarded as Important Cultural Properties by the government, the famous "Tabby Cat" by Takeuchi Seiho, and many works by Okamura Togyu.

● Ghibli Museum, Mitaka [Tokyo]

• 1-1-83 Shimorenjaku, Mitaka-shi, Tokyo • Adults: 1,000 yen, Age 13-18: 700 yen, Age 7-12: 400 yen, Age 4-6: 100 yen • **OPEN** 10am-6pm • **CLOSED** Tuesdays and Year-end & New Year holidays • http://www.ghibli-museum.jp • Museum shop, café, theater

Visitors can meet all Ghibli characters like Totoro and Nausica at this museum. Entrance is strictly by advance purchase of a reserved ticket with the appointed date at designated Lawson convenience store in Japan. Check the website for details.

● Tokyo Metropolitan Teien Art Museum [Tokyo]

- 5-21-9 Shirogane-dai, Minato-ku, Tokyo • Tel (+81) 3-3443-0201 • Adults: 200 yen, College: 160 yen • **OPEN** 10am-6pm • **CLOSED** the 2nd and 4th Wed of the month • http://www.teien-art-museum.ne.jp • Museum shop, café (the museum will be closed from Nov. 1, 2011 for upgrading.)

This Art Deco building was originally built in 1933 as the residence of the royal family and used for various state purposes until it was converted into a museum in 1983.

● Edo-Tokyo Museum [Tokyo]

- 1-4-1 Yokoami, Sumida-ku, Tokyo • Tel (+81) 3-3626-9974 • Adults: 600 yen, College: 480 yen • **OPEN** 9:30am-5:30pm • **CLOSED** Mondays • http://www.edo-tokyo-museum.or.jp • Museum shop, restaurant, audio-visual hall, library

The museum exhibits Tokyo's 400 years of history and culture. Its Edo zone, connected by the replica of Nihonbashi bridge, shows the daily life of people in Edo period. Tokyo zone shows how Edo has transformed into a modern city from the 19th century.

● The National Art Center, Tokyo [Tokyo]

- 7-22-2 Roppongi, Minato-ku, Tokyo • Tel (+81) 3-5777-8600 • Varies by exhibition • **OPEN** 10am-6pm, [Fri] 10am-8pm • **CLOSED** Tuesdays and Year-end/New Year holidays • http://www.nact.jp • Museum shop, restaurant, café, nursery service on selected dates

The museum has no permanent collection but provides its vast space for various exhibitions, large and small, including exhibitions by local art associations.

● Suntory Museum of Art [Tokyo]

- Tokyo Midtown Gardenside, 9-7-4 Akasaka, Minato-ku, Tokyo • Tel (+81) 3-3479-8600 • Varies by exhibition • **OPEN** [Wed-Sat] 10am-8pm, [Sun, Mon and public holidays] 10am-6pm • http://www.suntory.com • Museum shop, café

The museum, run by the major Japanese liquor maker Suntory, collects, houses and exhibits antique arts and crafts from Japan of over 4,000, including ukiyoe and old potteries, as old as 12th century (Kamakura period).

● Mori Art Museum [Tokyo]

- 53th Floor, Roppongi Hills Mori Tower, 6-10-1 Roppongi, Minato-ku, Tokyo • Tel (+81) 3-5777-8600 • Varies by exhibition • **OPEN** 10am-10pm, [Tue] 10am-5pm • http://www.mori.art.museum • Museum shop

The museum offers various educational activities to visitors, students and communities, including talks and workshops by young and promising artists. Located on the 53th floor, you can also enjoy the 360 degree view of Tokyo from the observatory.

● The Museum of Modern Art, Kamakura & Hayama [Kanagawa]

- 2208-1 Isshiki, Hayama-cho, Miura-gun, Kanagawa • Tel (+81) 46-875-2800
- Depend on exhibition • OPEN 9:30am-4:30pm • CLOSED Mondays, Year-end/New Year holidays, unfixed holiday • http://www.moma.pref.kanagawa.jp

Established in 1951, this is Japan's first public museum dedicated to early-modern art. The museum values ties with the local community, heritage, originality, and independence.

● The Hakone Open-Air Museum [Kanagawa]

- 1121 Ninotalra, Hakone-machi, Ashigarasimo-gun, Kanagawa • Tel (+81) 460-82-1161 • Adults: 1,600 yen, College/High school: 1,100 yen, Jr High/Elementary school: 800 yen • OPEN 9am-4:30pm • http://www.hakone-oam.or.jp • Restaurant, Museum shop, wedding

The museum was established in 1969 as the first open-air museum in Hakone. Some 120 pieces of contemporary sculpture are displayed around its vast garden.

● Hiroshima Peace Memorial Museum [Hiroshima]

- 1-2 Nakashima-cho, Naka-ku, Hiroshima • Tel (+81) 82-241-4004 • Adults: 50 yen, Elementary/Jr.High/High school: 30y en • OPEN 8:30am-5:30pm (Mar-Nov), 8:30am-16:30pm (Dec-Feb) • http://www.pcf.city.hiroshima.jp

Established in 1955, the museum aims to teach the catastrophe created by the atomic bombing of the city. Academics and the citizens of Hiroshima actively participated in collecting materials and the establishment of the museum from the beginning.

● Benesse Art Site Naoshima [Kagawa]

- Kototanchi, Naoshima-cho, Kagawa-gun, Kagawa • Tel (+81) 87-892-3223
- Adults: 1,000 yen, Age under 15 : Free • OPEN 8am-8pm • CLOSED Open Daily
- http://www.benesse-artsite.jp • Hotel, café, Museum shop, Restaurant

Benesse Art Site Naoshima both collects art works and provides artists and architects opportunities to create and exhibit their pieces on small islands in the Seto Inland Sea.

● The Isamu Noguchi Garden Museum Japan [Kagawa]

- 3519 Mure, Mure-cho, Takamatsu-shi, Kagawa • Tel (+81) 87-870-1500 • Adults: 2,100 yen • OPEN 10am, 1pm and 3pm on Tuesdays, Thursdays and Saturdays only
- http://www.isamunoguchi.or.jp • Museum shop

The museum was established by the will of Japanese-American architect, Isamu Noguchi. It includes 150 artworks, an archive, Noguchi's residence, and a sculpture garden. Admission is strictly by appointment at least 10 days in advance (details on website).

World Heritage Sites in Japan

Japan is a country of volcanic islands blessed with lush nature. It is also home to a population that has brewed its own traditions and external influences into a unique and sophisticated culture with a rich history. Efforts to protect the country's natural and cultural heritage for future generations have led to the designation of 16 sites as UNSECO World Heritage Sites.

● Buddhist Monuments in the Horyu-ji Area   Nara

• 1-1 Horyuji Sannai Ikaruga-cho, Ikoma-gun, Nara Prefecture 636-0115 • **Tel** (+81) 745-75-2555 • **OPEN** 8am-5pm (Feb.22-Nov.3), 8am-4:30pm (Nov.4-Feb.21) • http://www.horyuji.or.jp • Adults: 1,000 yen, Elementary school: 500 yen

Located in Nara Prefecture, Buddhist monuments in the Horyu-ji area hold artistic as well as historical importance. Among these 48 extraordinary monuments are some of the oldest surviving wooden buildings in the world, built in the late 7th or early 8th century. You can see architectural and the early Buddhist influence from China via Korea.

● Himeji-jo   Okayama

• Honmachi 68, Himeji, Hyogo • **Tel** (+81) 79-285-1146 • **OPEN** 9am-5pm (Apr.29-Aug.31), 9am-4pm (Sep.1-May.31) • http://www.city.himeji.lg.jp • Under construction for repairment until 2014. Parts of the castle can not be accessible. Please check the latest information before the visit • Adults: 400 yen, Elementary and Jr. High school: 100 yen

Himeji-jo is one of the finest surviving castles from the early 17th century. Built at an important communication center, this beautiful wooden architecture demonstrates the Japanese esthetic and skill for carefully planned function.

● Shirakami-Sanchi   Aomori / Akita

• http://www.city.himeji.lg.jp

The Shirakami mountains situated in the northern Honshu extend over 450km2 of the untouched Siebold's beech forest and deep valleys. Rich fauna of animals and insect species live among more than 500 plant species, most of them unique to the country. This undisturbed wilderness is surrounded and protected by a buffer zone, with no accessible trails or man-made facilities .

● Yakushima [Kagoshima]

• http://whc.unesco.org

Yakushima, or Yaku Island, is located in the northern tip of the Ryukyu archipelago, off the shore of Kyushu Island. The central region is mountainous, with many ridges over 1800m high, and features the highest mountain in Kyushu region. A warm climate with abundant rain has created a unique flora. The most famous example of this is yakusugi, a type of Japanese cedar with an extremely long life span, the oldest of which is confirmed to be over 3,000 years old.

● Historic Monuments of Ancient Kyoto (Kyoto, Uji and Otsu Cities)

• kyototourismcouncil@yahoo.co.jp • http://www.kyoto.travel/ [Kyoto / Shiga]

Modeled after the ancient Chinese capital, Kyoto was the imperial capital of Japan from its founding in 749 A.D. until the mid-19th century. During this time, Japanese wooden architecture, especially religious buildings, art gardens, and many masterpieces were built all around Kyoto. Properties inscribed on the World Heritage List include 13 Buddhist temples, 3 Shinto shrines, and a castle. Each site represents its own period and, needless to say, possesses breathtaking beauty.

● Historic Villages of Shirakawa-go and Gokayama [Gifu / Toyama]

• #501-56 Hatotani-517 Shirakawa-Village Ohno-District Gifu Pref • Tel (+81) 5769-6-1311 • http://shirakawa-go.org/english/index.html

Isolated in the deep mountainous region, the historic villages of Shirakawa-go and Gokayama kept their unique and traditional Gassho-style houses and way of life in perfect harmony with the beautiful local environment. You will feel like you have wondered into a world of folk tales in this remote humble village with unique triangle-shaped houses where people still live today.

● Hiroshima Peace Memorial (Genbaku Dome) [Hiroshima]

• 1-2 Nakajimama-cho, Naka-ku, Hiroshima City 730-0811, Japan • Tel (+81) 82-242-7798 • OPEN 8:30am-6pm (Mar.1-Nov.30), 8:30am-5pm (Dec.1-Feb.28), 8:30am-7pm (Aug.1-31) • http://www.pcf.city.hiroshima.jp • Adults: 50 yen, Age 6-18: 30 yen

The Hiroshima Peace Memorial (Genbaku Dome) is a powerful symbol of people's hope for peace and stands as the witness of brutality of war and the atomic bomb. It was the only structure standing after the atomic bombing of the city on August 6th, 1945, and was preserved through the effort of many in the hope of never repeating the same tragedy.

● Itsukushima-jinja   `Hiroshima`

- 1-11-1 Shimohera, Hatsukaichi-shi, Hiroshima 738-8501   • **Tel** (+81) 829-30-9141
- **OPEN** 6:30am-6pm   • http://www.miyajima-island.com   • Adults: 300 yen, High school: 200 yen, Elementary and Jr.High school: 100 yen

Itsukushima (Miyajima), an island in Seto Inland Sea off of Hiroshima, has been a holy place of Shintoism since the early times. The shrine (Itsukushima-jinja) is believed to be built in 593 originally but the current shrine was built in the middle of 12th century. The shrine and the gates are holding its place in the sea entirely by its own weight, and superb skill was put into build this beautiful scenic shrine to worship and respect nature.

● Historic Monuments of Ancient Nara   `Nara`

- **Tel** (+81) 742-27-8477   • http://www.pref.nara.jp

The city's historic monuments – BuddhiNara served as the capital of Japan from 710 to 784. Even after the capital moved to Kyoto and much of the city was abandoned, many Buddhist temples and shrines in Nara maintained their high status and imperial patronage. Among them, 5 Buddhist temples, a Shinto shrine and a palace, and a primeval forest are registered as the World Heritage site, all of which were originally built during the Nara period or even earlier and transferred to the city when it became the capita. They include Todai-ji with the 15-meter high magnificent bronze statue of the Great Buddha and Gango-ji, the oldest Buddhist temple in the country.

● Shrines and Temples of Nikko   `Tochigi`

- **Tel** (+81) 288-22-1111   • http://www.city.nikko.lg.

The shrines and temples of Nikko are magnificent architectural masterpieces built in harmony with the beautiful nature of the sacred Nikko mountain. Thought the first buildings were erected in the 8th century, Nikko gained the important role of as a symbol of national sovereignty when it was chosen to house the mausoleum of Tokugawa Ieyasu, the founder of 250-year long Tokugawa shogunate. Their accessible location allows a day trip to escape the busy streets of Tokyo to enjoy the extraordinary architecture and the serene nature.

● Gusuku Sites and Related Properties of the Kingdom of Ryukyu

- **Tel** (+81) 98-866-2333   • okinawa@pref.okinawa.lg.jp
- http://www.pref.okinawa.jp   `Okinawa`

Ryuku (Okinawa) was an important economic as well as cultural intersection of Southeast Asian countries in its history (12th-17th century). Preceding to its unification in 1429, powerful communities surrounded themselves with stone walls which later developed into castles (gusuku). Together with mitaki, sacred places of the unique religion in Okinawa, the gusuku show the remains of the rich culture of the Kingdom of Ryukyu.

🔵 Sacred Sites and Pilgrimage Routes in the Kii Mountain Range

• hkishu@pref.mie.jp • http://www.pref.mie.lg.jp | Mie / Nara / Wakayama |

The Sacred Sites and Pilgrimage routes are hidden in the dense forests of the Kii Mountains surrounded by the Pacific Ocean. A narrow path links three sacred sites, Yoshino and Omine, Kumano Sanzan, and Koyasan, has attracted a large number of worshippers since the 11th or 12th century. These sites show a unique fusion of Shintoism and Buddhism, and influenced the building of temples and shrines all over Japan.

🔵 Shiretoko | Hokkaido |

• **Tel** (+81) 152-24-2114 • http://www.shiretoko.or.jp

Located in northeast Hokkaido, Shiretoko Peninsula exhibits a stunning interaction between the ecologies of a number of marine and terrestrial species, some of which are endangered and endemic.

🔵 Iwami Ginzan Silver Mine and its Cultural Landscape

• **Tel** (+81) 854-89-0183 • http://ginzan.city.ohda.lg.jp | Shimane |

The Iwami Ginzan Silver Mine, located in the mountains of Shimane prefecture in the southwest of Honshu Island, once produced a third of silver in the world. With highly developed skills and efficiently organized mining sites, settlement, transportation and shipping routes, and a fortress, the area produced massive amounts of high-quality silver while preserving the surrounding nature.

🔵 Hiraizumi – Temples, Gardens and Archaeological Sites Representing the Buddhist Pure Land | Shimane |

• **Tel** (+81) 191-46-2110 • http://hiraizumi.or.jp

Hiraizumi was founded by Fujiwara no Kiyohira and served as the administrative center of the northern Japan from late 11th century to late 12th century. Based on the cosmology of Pure Land Buddhism, it was built to represent the pure land of Buddha, for the dead to reach it and for the living to get a peace of mind.

🔵 Ogasawara Islands | Tokyo |

• **Tel** (+81) 4998-2-2587 • http://www.ogasawaramura.com

Ogasawara Islands consists of over 30 islands in the Pacific approximately 1000km Southeast of Tokyo. These virtually untouched islands host a rich wealth of fauna and a large number of endangered birds. The surrounding ocean supports numerous species of fish, cetaceans, and corals.

● Katsura Imperial Villa [Kyoto]

• Katsura Misono, Nishigyo-ku, Kyoto-shi, Kyoto • [Rail] Hankyu Kyoto Line, Katsura station. [Bus] Bus no. 33, Katsura-rikyu stop • To visit Katsura Imperial Villa should apply for permission in accordance with the guidelines. http://sankan.kunaicho.go.jp

Katsura-rikyu is a world famous imperial villa featuring a simple, but functional architectural style. It has the original sukiya-style shoin or study room consisting of three sections – Ko-shoin, Chu-shoin, and Shin-goten – with a circuit-style garden and a tearoom.

● Shugakuin Imperial Villa [Kyoto]

• Shugakuin Yabuzoe, Sakyo-ku, Kyoto-shi, Kyoto • [Rail] Eizan Dentetsu Line, Shugakuin sta. [Bus] Bus no. 5, Shugaku-in Rikyumichi stop • To visit Shugakuin Imperial Villa should apply for permission in accordance with the guidelines. http://sankan.kunaicho.go.jp

Shugakuin-rikyu Imperial Villa sits on vast grounds (approximately 540,000 square meters) complete with arable fields, achieving peacefulness and nobleness. Its magnificent and graceful gardens feature scenery of its backdrop, Mt. Shugakuin.

● Ise-jingu [Mie]

• Ujiyakata-cho, Ise-shi, Mie • Kintetsu Line, Uji-yamada station, or JR Line, Ise station • Free in the shrine precincts • http://www.isejingu.or.jp

Ise Jingu in Mie Prefecture is sacred to Amaterasu Sumera O-mikami, the sun goddess. Its Shikinen Sengu, the ceremonious installation of deity in a new shrine, takes place once every 20 years, when necessary buildings are rebuilt in adjacent grounds. The first ceremony was performed in 690, and has continued for 1,300 years.

● Izumo-taisha [Shimane]

• 195 Kizuki-higashi, Taisha-cho, Izumo-shi, Shimane • Ichibata Dentetsu Line, Izumo-Taisha-Mae station • **OPEN** 6am-8pm, Open Daily • [Shrine] free [Treasure house] 150 yen [Shokokan] 50 yen • http://www.izumooyashiro.or.jp

The Izumo-Taisha is located in eastern Shimane. According to the myth in the Izumo district, the god of fortune obtained Izumo in compensation for giving his territory to another god. It also has O-torii, the largest shrine gate in Japan, and a huge sacred straw festoon.

● Itsukushima-jinja [Hiroshima]

• 1-1 Miyajimacho, Hatsukaichi-shi, Hiroshima • JR Sanyo Line, Miyajima-guchi station, and to Miyajima by ferry • www.miyajima-wch.jp

Located off the coast of Hiroshima, the island of Itsukushima or Miyajima has been considered a holy place for most of Japanese history. Itsukushima-jinja is a large, red-lacquered complex of halls and pathways on stilts along with its famous gateway, Otorii. The Shrine and the Otorii together are designated a UNESCO World Heritage Site.

● Kasuga-taisha Nara

• 160 Kasugano-cho, Nara-shi, Nara • About 15 min walk from Kintetsu Nara station. [Bus] Kasuga-taishamae Stop • **OPEN** 6:30am-5:30pm (Apr-Oct), 7am-4:30pm (Nov-Mar) • [Main hall] 500 yen [Museun] 400 yen • http://www.kasugataisha.or.jp

Kasuga Taisha is one of the three greatest shrines of Japan, founded during the Nara Period (710-794). It lies at the foot of two sacred mountains from which the Shinto gods first descended.

● Fushimi-Inari-taisha Kyoto

• 68 Yabunouchi-cho, Fukakusa Fushimi-ku, Kyoto-shi, Kyoto • JR Nara Line, JR Inari station or Keihan line, Fushimiinari station • **OPEN** 8:30am-4:30pm • Free

The Fushimi-Inari Taisha is believed to have been built to worship the god of rice and sake in the 8th century. As centuries went on, the god also came to be known as the one to ensure prosperity in business. Often called "Oinari-san", it is the head shrine of no fewer than 30,000 Inari branch shrines nationwide today.

● Heian-jingu Kyoto

• Nishi Tennocho, Okazaki, Sakyo-ku, Kyoto-shi, Kyoto • Bus no. 5 to Kyoto Kalkan Bijitusukan-mae stop • **OPEN** 6am-5:30pm (Mar, Sep), 6am-6pm (Apr-Aug), 6am-5pm (Nov-Feb) • [Garden] Adults: 600 yen/Children: 300 yen • www.helanjingu.or.jp

It was established in 1895 to celebrate the 1,100th anniversary of the foundation of the capital of Heian. Its buildings are 2/3-sized partial replicas of the ancient Heian Imperial palace.

● Jishu-jinja Kyoto

• 1-317 Klyomizu, Higashiyama-ku, Kyoto-shi, Kyoto • Bus no. 201, 100. 201, about 10 min walk from Gojozaka stop or Kiyomizu-michi stop • **OPEN** 9am-5pm • Free • http://www.jishujinja.or.jp

Jishu-jinja in Kyoto is so old that the sacred rock of good marriage at the shrine dates back to prehistoric time. Today. it is known for bringing good marriage and is always surrounded by a crowd of young women praying for "The One".

● Nikko Toshogu Nikko

• 2301 Sannai, Nikko-shi, Tochigi • A 30-40min walk from JR Nikko and Tobu Nikko station • **OPEN** 8am-5pm (Apr-Oct), 8am-4pm (Nov-Mar) • Adults: 1,300 yen, Children: 450 yen • www.nikko-jp.org/english/toshogu

Nikko Toshogu is a Shinto shrine and the mausoleum of Tokugawa Ieyasu, who founded the Edo Shogunate. The engravings on the Yomei-mon Gate are especially famous for their gorgeous colors. The three monkeys and the sleeping cat are also famous.

● Meiji-jingu Tokyo

• 1-1 Yoyogikamizono-cho, Shibuya-ku, Tokyo • JR Yamanote Line, Harajuku station, Chiyoda Line/Fukutoshi Line, Meijijingumae station • **OPEN** Open Daily, opens with sunrise and closes with sunset • Free • www.meijijingu.or.jp

Though surrounded by modern buildings of fashionable Harajuku and Shibuya, you may feel as if you wondered into a different world when you step into the lush forest of Meiji Jingu, a shrine dedicated to the deified spirits of Emperor Meiji.

● Tsurugaoka Hachimangu Shrine Kamakura

• 2-1-31 Yukinoshita, Kamakura-shi, Kanagawa • A 10min walk from the JR Kamakura station • **OPEN** 6:30am-9pm • Free • http://www.hachimangu.or.jp

As a symbol of Kamakura, this Shinto shrine has attracted many visitors since its founding in the 12th century. On its grounds, there are the treasure house, pond-gardens, and a huge gingko tree said to be more than 1,000 years old. On top of the 61 stone steps leading up to the main shrine is a magnificent view of Kamakura.

● Chuson-ji Iwate

• Hiraizumi, Hiraizumi-cho, Nishi-Iwai-gun, Iwate • Take bus no. 4 from JR Hiraizumi station to Chuson-ji stop • 8:30am-5pm (Mar-Nov.3), 8:30am-4:30pm (Nov.4-Feb) • 800 yen, Open Daily • http://www.chusonji.or.jp

The Konjiki-do of Chuson-ji, built by the Fujiwaras, is decorated inside and out with lacquer containing gold foil and studded with gold and silver, a symbol of the gold culture of Hiraizumi. Chuson-ji was recognized by UNESCO as a World Cultural Heritage in 2011.

● Zenko-ji Nagano

• 491 Motyoshi-cho, Nagano-shi, Nagano • Nagano station by JR Nagano Shinkansen Line • 24 hour • Free, [Main Hall] Adults: 500 yen, High school: 200 yen, Jr. High/Elementary School: 50 yen • http://www.zenkoji.jp

Zenko-ji, built in the early 7th century, is a popular tourist spot in Nagano with a never-ending line of visitors. The temple is famous for its involvement in a famous battle between two powerful warriors in the 16th century.

● Horyu-ji Nara

• 1-1 Horyu-ji Sannai, Ikaruga-cho, Ikoma-gun, Nara • JR Kansai Line, Horyu-ji sta., or take bus form Ohji sta. to Horyu-ji gate stop • **OPEN** 8am-5pm (Feb.22-Nov.3), 8am-4:30pm (Nov.4-Feb.21) • Adults: 1,000 yen, Elementary School: 500 yen • www.horyuji.or.jp

Horyu-ji is a Buddhist temple featuring one of the world's oldest surviving wooden structures. Several of its structures and their contents are listed as National Treasures.

⦿ Kofuku-ji Nara

• 48 Noborioji-cho, Nara-shi, Nara • A 7 min. walk from Kintetsu Nara station. Or city loop bus No. 2, Kencho-mae stop • **OPEN** 9am-5pm, Open Daily • [National Treasure Museum] Adults: 600 yen • www.kohfukuji.com

Kofuku-ji is one of Japan's most celebrated Buddhist temples. The temple was established in 710, the year when Nara became the capital, and is now a UNESCO World Heritage Site. The temple was founded by the powerful Fujiwara clan.

⦿ Todai-ji Nara

• 1 Zoshi-cho, Nara-shi, Nara • A 15min walk from Kintetsu Nara station • **OPEN** 7:30am-5:30pm (Apr-Sep), 7:30am-5pm (Oct), 8am-4:30pm (Nov-Feb), 8am-5pm (Mar) • [Daibutsu-den Hall] 500 yen • http://www.todaiji.or.jp

Todai-ji, one of the most famous Buddhist temples and a landmark of Nara, was consecrated in 752 when Nara was the capital. The Great Buddha of Nara, a 15-meter tall bronze and copper masterpiece, sits majestically in the grand Daibutsu-den.

⦿ Saiho-ji (Kokedera) Kyoto

• 56 Matsuo-Jingatani-cho, Nishikyo-ku, Kyoto-shi, Kyoto • Kyoto Bus, Kokedera-michi Stop • 3,000 yen, Advanced reservations are required

The garden of Saiho-ji, one of Kyoto's most famous gardens, is believed to have been created in the 14th century by Muso Kokushi, a master gardener. The garden is covered by over 120 different species of moss, creating an illusionary and tranquil ambience in rich green, making the temple known as Koke-dera – "the temple of moss".

⦿ Daigo-ji Kyoto

• 22 Higashi-Oji-cho, Fushimi-ku, Kyoto-shi, Kyoto • JR Biwako Line, Yamashina sta. and Kyoto City Subway Tozai Line, Daigo station • **OPEN** 9am-5pm (Mar-Dec), 9am-4pm (Dec-Feb) • 1,500 yen for all of buildings • http://www.daigoji.or.jp

Daigo-san, a World Cultural Heritage established in the 9th century, is one of the largest temples in Kyoto. Its buildings, including many National Treasures and Important Cultural Properties, are spread around the entire mountain of Daigo-san.

⦿ Tofuku-ji Kyoto

• 15-778 Honmachi, Higashiyama-ku, Kyoto-shi, Kyoto • JR Nara Line, Tofukuji station. Bus No. 202/207/208, Tofukuji Bus Stop • **OPEN** 9am-4am (Apr-Oct), 8:30am-4pm (Nov-Dec), 9am-3:30pm (Dec-Mar), Open Daily • [Hojo Hasso Garden] 400 yen • http://www.tofukuji.jp

Tofuku-ji is a Zen temple built in mid-13th century. Of the four gardens surrounding the temple, the northern garden with moss and stones is particularly famous.

🔴 Koryu-ji Kyoto

- 32 Uzumasa-Hachioka-cho, Ukyo-ku, Kyoto-shi, Kyoto • [Rail] Keifuku Arashiyama Line or JR Sagano Line, Uzumasa station [Bus] No. 11/75/91/93, Uzumasa-Koryuji-mae stop • [Reiho-den] 700 yen [Keigu-in Hondo] 200 yen

Koryu-ji is an ancient temple established in early 7th century. It houses ancient Buddhist statues, including the Miroku-Bosatsu-zo (a Bodhisattva who is supposed to be the successor of the Buddha in the future world), the first designated National Treasure.

🔴 Ryoan-ji Kyoto

- 13 Ryoan-ji Goryonoshita-cho, Ukyo-ku, Kyoto-shi, Kyoto • Bus no. 50/55, Ritsumeikan Univ.-mae stop. no. 59, Ryoanji-mae Stop • **OPEN** 8am-5am (Mar-Nov), 8:30am-4:30pm (Dec-Feb), Open Daily • 500 yen • http://www.ryoanji.jp

The garden at Ryoan-ji Hojo is one of Kyoto's most famous. The white sand covering the oblong garden is raked into a ripple pattern, and 15 rocks are exquisitely positioned with one rock always hidden regardless of the angle, creating a sense of infinite expanse.

🔴 Kinkaku-ji Kyoto

- 1 Kinkaku-ji, Kita-ku, Kyoto-shi, Kyoto • Bus no. 59, Kinkakuji-mae stop, bus no. 59/101/102/204/205, Kinkaku-ji-michi stop • **OPEN** 9am-5pm • Adults: 400 yen, Children: 300 yen • http://www.shokoku-ji.or.jp/kinkakuji/

Officially named Rokuon-ji, Kinkaku-ji is perhaps the most famous sight in Kyoto. Visitors can savor the gold-covered pavilion and its beautiful reflection on the "mirror pond" scattered with exquisite rock islands and pine trees.

🔴 Daitoku-ji Kyoto

- 53 Murasakino-Daitokuji-cho, Kita-ku, Kyoto-shi, Kyoto • Bus no. 1/12/101/102/ 204/205/206/Kita-8, Daitokuji-mae stop • http://zen.rinnou.net/

Originally built in the 14th century and subsequently restored by the famous priest Ikkyu after a fire, Daitoku-ji is the biggest temple in Kyoto. The Zuiho-in subtemple, established by a Christian daimyo, is noted for the cross made from seven stones that extend across its Karesansui, a garden wherein nature is expressed with stones and sand.

🔴 Kiyomizu-dera Kyoto

- 1-294 Kiyomizu, Higashiyama-ku, Kyoto-shi, Kyoto • [Bus] no. 100/206/207, Gojo-zaka stop • **OPEN** 6am-6pm • Adults: 300 yen, Jr. High and Elementary school: 200 yen • http://www.kiyomizudera.or.jp

Kiyomizu-dera, a temple dating to the late 8th century and registered World Heritage Site, has been adored for hundreds of years. The Hondo (Main Hall) is noted for its outstanding background scenery which changes with seasons.

● Nanzen-ji   Kyoto

• Nanzenji-Fukuchi-cho, Sakyo-ku, Kyoto-shi, Kyoto   • [Bus] no. 5, Nanzenji Eikando-michi stop [Subway] Tozai Line, Keage station   • **CLOSED** Dec. 28-31   • [Hojo Garden] 500 yen   • http://www.nanzen.com

Nanzen-ji, also called Zuiryusan, is one of the most well-known Rinzai Zen temples in Japan. Emperor Kameyama loved this beautiful place so much that he built his detached palace here in 1264.

● Ginkaku-ji   Kyoto

• 2 Ginkakuji-cho, Sakyo-ku, Kyoto-shi, Kyoto   • A 10 min walk from Keihan Demachi-yanagi station, or a 5 min walk from Ginkakuji-mae city bus stop   • **OPEN** 8:30am-5pm   • Adults: 500 yen, Children: 300 yen   • http://www.shokoku-ji.or.jp/ginkakuji/

The Ginkaku-ji, or Temple of the Silver Pavilion, is a better-known name for the Jisho-ji, which belongs to the Buddhist Shokoku School of the Rinzai Zen Sect. The temple is located in the Higashiyama District at the foot of Kyoto's eastern mountains.

● Sanjusangendo   Kyoto

• 657 Sanjusangenndo-mawarimachi, Higashiyama-ku, Kyoto-shi, Kyoto   • 5 min walk from Keihan-Shichijo sta., or take City bus to Hakubutsukan-sanjusangendo-mae stop   • **OPEN** 8am-5pm (Apr-Nov.15), 9am-4pm (Nov.16-Mar.31)   • Adults: 600 yen, Students: 400 yen, Children: 300 yen   • http://sanjusangendo.jp

Rengeo-in, known by its nickname "Sanjusangen-do" (a hall with 33 spaces between the columns), features 1,001 figures of the Kannon Goddess from the 12th and 13th centuries.

● To-ji   Kyoto

• 1 Kujo-cho, Minami-ku, Kyoto-shi, Kyoto   • A 15 min walk from JR Kyoto station and Kintetsu Kyoto Line, Kintetsu Kyoto Line, Toji station   • **OPEN** 8:30am-5:30pm (Mar.20-Sep.19), 8:30am-4:30pm (Sep.20 -Mar.19)   • 500 yen   • http://www.toji.or.jp

To-ji, established in the 8th century, has a symbolic 53-meter tall five-storied pagoda. A special ceremony and a 500-year-old open-air market on the 21st of the month commemorate the high priest Kobo Daishi.

● Byodo-in   Kyoto

• Uji-renge, Uji-shi, Kyoto   • Keihan Uji station, JR Uji station   • **OPEN** 9:30am-4pm [Garden] 8:30-5pm [Museum] 9am-5pm   • 600 yen   • http://www.byodoin.or.jp

Byodo-in, on the west bank of the Uji-gawa River, was once a villa of the Fujiwara clan until it was turned into a temple in the mid-11th century. Ho-o-do Hall across Ajiga Pond is a National Treasure. It was constructed as a way to realize the paradise that the nobles at that time dreamed about.

● Enryaku-ji `Shiga`

• 4220 Sakamoto honmachi, Otsu-shi, Shiga • Take bus from JR Kyoto sta. 1-hour ride to Enryaku-ji stop • Hour & Fee : Check website for details • http://www.hieizan.or.jp

Enryaku-ji is the headquarters of the Tendai sect and was opened in 785 by Saicho. The temple property is dotted with more than 100 buildings and towers, including the Konpon-chudo, a National Treasure, a large lecture hall, and Shaka-do, all shaded by a forest of ancient Japanese cedar trees.

● Kongobu-ji `Wakayama`

• 132 Koyasan, Koya-cho, Ito-gun, Wakayama • Nankai Koyasan Cable, from Nankai-Gokuraku-bashi sta. to Koyasan sta. and take bus to Kongobu-ji-mae stop • **OPEN** 8:30am-5pm • Ticket for all of the buildings: 1500 yen • http://www.koyasan.or.jp

Kobo Daishi (Kukai) of the 8th century studied Buddhism in Tang-dynasty China. When he returned, he founded Shingon sect and established Kongobu-ji on Mt. Koya.

● Senso-ji `Tokyo`

• 2-3-1 Asakusa, Taito-ku, Tokyo • Ginza Line or Toei Asakusa Line, Asakusa station • Free, Open Daily • http://www.senso-ji.jp

Senso-ji, one of the best known sights in Tokyo, dates back to 628 A.D. According to a legend, two brothers found an image of Kannon Goddess in Sumida River and held a religious service here. The famous Kaminari-mon (Thunder Gate) features large images of Fujin (God of Wind) and Raijin (God of Thunder), which gives the gate its name.

● Shuzen-ji `Shizuoka`

• 964 Shuzenji, Izu-shi, Shizuoka • Izu-Hakone Sunzu Line, Mishima to Shuzenji station, and take bus from the station.

Shuzen-ji is a hot spring resort located on a hill surrounded by scenic mountains in the Izu Peninsula. Legend has it that Kobo-Daishi, the great monk of the 8th century, brought forth the hot spring water with his walking stick. He also erected Oku-no-in on the beautiful temple grounds of Shuzen-ji, where he received training in his youth.

● Hase-dera `Kamakura`

• 3-11-2 Hase, Kamakura-shi, Kanagawa • Enoden line from JR Kamakura station to Hase station • **OPEN** 8am-5:30pm (Mar-Sep), 8am-5pm (Oct-Feb) • 300 yen • http://www.hasedera.jp

A wide variety of flowers, changing with the seasons, bloom on the grounds of this temple: peonies, hydrangeas, fragrant olives, camellias, and many more. Sited high on a hill, you can enjoy a fine view from the main temple.

● **Hokoku-ji** `Kamakura`

• 2-7-4 Jomyo-ji, Kamakura-shi, Kanagawa • A 25 min walk from JR Kamakura station, or take Keikyu bus to Jyomoji stop • **OPEN** 9am-4pm • 200 yen

Hokoku-ji is a Zen temple founded in the 14th century. Behind the temple is a magnificent garden where bamboo stalks grow incredibly close together and shoot straight into to the sky. Breathe in the sacred silence and serene air of this wonderful garden.

● **Kencho-ji** `Kamakura`

• 8 Yamanouchi, Kamakura-shi, Kanagawa • About 15min walk from JR Kita-Kamakura station • **OPEN** 8:30am-4:30pm • 300 yen • www.kenchoji.com

Kencho-ji is one of the most important medieval Zen temples in Kamakura, overlooking the city all the way to Sagami Bay. Two gates, the Buddhist sanctum, a lecture hall, and a hut are all built along a straight line with quiet dignity. Behind the temple grounds stands Hansobo, a shrine dedicated to a Shinto deity that protects the temple.

● **Kamakura Daibutsu-den** `Kamakura`

• 4-2-28 Hase, Kamakura-shi, Kanagawa • Take the Enoden line from JR Kamakura station to Hase station • **OPEN** 7am-6pm (Apr-Sep), 7am-5:30pm (Oct-Mar) • Adults: 200 yen, Children: 150 yen • http://www.kotoku-in.jp

Though this 11m-tall bronze statue of Buddha is a symbolic figure of Kamakura, its origin is largely unknown. Once covered with gold and housed in a grand building in the 13th century, the statue now sits elegantly in the open air.

● **Engaku-ji** `Kamakura`

• 409 Yamanouchi, Kamakura-shi, Kanagawa • Few min walk from JR Kita-Kamakura station • **OPEN** 8am-5pm (Apr-Oct), 8am-4am (Nov-Mar) • 300 yen • http://www. engakuji.or.jp

Enkaku-ji is one of the major Zen temples in Kamakura and is located right next to Kita-Kamakura Station. Nestled on a hill deeply forested with cedar trees, the temple grounds have an otherworldly tranquil atmosphere.

● **Chikurin-ji** `Kochi`

• 3577 Godaisan, Kochi-shi, Kochi • About 26 min from Kochi station to Chikurin-ji-mae stop by MY-YOU bus • http://www.chikurinji.com

Chikuren-ji was established based on a dream of Emperor Shomua in 724. Kobo Daishi, a great monk of the 8th century, supposedly visited and trained here. During the Edo period, it was one of the leading temples in the region.

● Hotel & Resort Mashio `Oshima Island/Tokyo`

• 492-1 Ohora, Motomachi, Oshima-machi, Tokyo • TEL (+81) 4992-2-7317 • 3 rooms • http://www.mashio.com • VISA / MASTER / JCB / AMEX / DINERS • Room with open-air bath

● The Capitol Hotel Tokyu `Nagatacho/Tokyo`

• 2-10-3 Nagata-cho, Chiyoda-ku, Tokyo • TEL (+81) 3-3503-0109 • 251 rooms • http://www.capitolhoteltokyu.com • VISA / MASTER / JCB / AMEX / DINERS / UNION PAY • Indoor pool, fitness facility

● Mandarin Oriental Tokyo `Nihonbashi/Tokyo`

• 2-1-1, Nihonbashi-Muromachi, Chuo-ku, Tokyo • TEL (+81) 3-3270-8800 • 178 rooms • http://www.mandarinoriental.com • VISA / MASTER / JCB / AMEX / DINERS / UNION PAY

● Conrad Tokyo `Shiodome/Tokyo`

• 1-9-1 Higashi-Shinbashi, Minato-ku, Tokyo • TEL (+81) 3-6388-8000 • 290 rooms • http://conradtokyo.co.jp • VISA / MASTER / JCB / AMEX / DINERS • Indoor pool, fitness facility

● The Ritz-Carlton, Tokyo `Roppongi/Tokyo`

• Tokyo Midtown, 9-7-1, Akasaka, Minato-ku, Tokyo • TEL (+81) 3-3423-8000 • 245 rooms • http://www.ritzcarlton.com • VISA / MASTER / JCB / AMEX / DINERS • Indoor pool, fitness facility

● Grand Hyatt Tokyo `Roppongi/Tokyo`

• 6-10-3 Roppongi, Minato-ku, Tokyo • TEL (+81) 3-4333-1234 • 389 rooms • http://tokyo.grand.hyatt.jp • VISA / MASTER / JCB / AMEX / DINERS • Indoor pool, fitness facility

● Four Seasons Hotel Chinzanso `Mejiro/Tokyo`

• 2-10-8 Sekiguchi, Bunkyo-ku, Tokyo • TEL (+81) 3-3943-7070 • 259 rooms • http://www.fourseasons-tokyo.com • VISA / MASTER / JCB / AMEX / DINERS • Indoor pool, fitness facility, onsen

● Shangri-La Hotel, Tokyo `Marunouchi/Tokyo`

• Marunouchi Trust Tower Main Bldg., 1-8-3 Marunouchi, Chiyoda-ku, Tokyo • **TEL** (+81) 3-6739-7888 • 200 rooms • http://www.shangri-la.com • VISA / MASTER / JCB / AMEX / DINERS / UNION PAY • Indoor pool, fitness facility

● Four Seasons Hotel Marunouchi `Marunouchi/Tokyo`

• Pacific Century Place Marunouchi, 1-11-1 Marunouchi, Chiyoda-ku, Tokyo • **TEL** (+81) 3-5222-7222 • 57 rooms • http://www.fourseasons.com • VISA / MASTER / JCB / AMEX / DINERS • Onsen, fitness facility

● Imperial Hotel Tokyo `Hibiya/Tokyo`

• 1-1-1 Uchisaiwaicho, Chiyoda-ku, Tokyo • **TEL** (+81) 3-3504-1111 • 931 rooms • http://www.imperialhotel.co.jp • VISA / MASTER / JCB / AMEX / DINERS • Indoor pool, fitness facility, nursery room

● The Peninsula Tokyo `Hibiya/Tokyo`

• 1-8-1 Yurakucho, Chiyoda-ku, Tokyo • **TEL** (+81) 3-6270-2888 • 314 rooms • http://www.peninsula.com • VISA / MASTER / JCB / AMEX / DINERS / UNION PAY • Indoor pool, fitness facility

● Hotel New Otani `Akasakamituke/Tokyo`

• 4-1 Kioicho, Chiyoda-ku, Tokyo • **TEL** (+81) 3-3265-1111 • http://www.newotani. co.jp • VISA / MASTER / JCB / AMEX / DINERS • Outdoor pool, fitness facility, nursery room, free pick up service

● Hotel Okura Tokyo `Toranomon/Tokyo`

• 2-10-4 Toranomon, Minato-ku, Tokyo • **TEL** (+81) 3-3582-0111 • 801 rooms • http://www.hotelokura.co.jp • VISA / MASTER / AMEX / DINERS / JCB • Outdoor pool (seasonal), indoor pool, fitness facility, spa

● The Agnes Hotel and Apartments Tokyo `Tokyo/Iidabashi`

• 2-20-1 Kagurazaka, Shinjuku-ku, Tokyo • **TEL** (+81) 3-3267-5505 • 56 rooms • http://www.agneshotel.com • VISA / MASTER / JCB / AMEX / DINERS • Restaurant, Access to Kagurazaka district

● Park Hyatt Tokyo `Nishi-Shinjuku/Tokyo`

• 3-7-1-2 Nishi-Shinjuku, Shinjuku-ku, Tokyo • **TEL** (+81) 3-5322-1234 • 177 rooms • http:/parkhyatttokyo.com • VISA / MASTER / JCB / AMEX / DINERS • Indoor pool, fitness facility, free pick up service

● The Westin Tokyo `Ebisu/Tokyo`

• 1-4-1 Mita, Meguro-ku, Tokyo • **TEL** (+81) 3-5423-7770 • 432 rooms • http://www.starwoodhotels.com • VISA / MASTER / JCB / AMEX / DINERS / UNION PAY • Fitness facility

● CLASKA `Meguro/Tokyo`

• 1-3-18 Chuo-cho, Meguro-ku, Tokyo • **TEL** (+81) 3-3719-8121 • 18 rooms • http://www.claska.com • VISA / MASTER / JCB / AMEX / DINERS • Tatami rooms

● Kouunkan `Gunma (Ikaho Onsen)`

• 175-1 Ikaho, Ikaho-machi, Shibukawa-shi, Gunma • **TEL** (+81) 279-72-5501 • 10 rooms • http://www.kouunkan.jp • VISA / MASTER / JCB / AMEX / DINERS • Japanese-style inn, onsen, room with open-air bath

● Tenojiya `Gunma (Kusatsu Onsen)`

• 360 Kusatsu, Kusatsumachi, Agatsuma-gun, Gunma • **TEL** (+81) 279-88-3177 • 12 rooms • http://www.tenojiya.co.jp • VISA / MASTER / JCB / AMEX / DINERS • Japanese-style inn, onsen, open-air bath

● Nikko Kanaya Hotel `Tochigi`

• 1300 Kamihatsuishi-machi, Nikko-shi, Tochigi • **TEL** (+81) 288-54-0001 • 71 rooms • http://www.kanayahotel.co.jp • VISA / MASTER / JCB / AMEX / DINERS • Outdoor pool (seasonal), Ice skate rink (seasonal)

● Chuzenji Kanaya Hotel `Nikko/Tochigi`

• 2482 Chugushi, Nikko-shi, Tochigi • **TEL** (+81) 288-51-0001 • 59 rooms • http://www.kanayahotel.co.jp • VISA / AMEX / DINERS / JCB • Onsen, open-air bath, free pick up service

● Bandaisan Onsen Hotel   `Fukushima`

- 6838-68 Shimizudaira, Sarashina, Bandai-machi, Yama-gun, Fukushima   • **TEL** (+81) 242-74-5100 • 152 rooms • http://www.bandaisan.co.jp • VISA / MASTER / JCB / AMEX / DINERS • Onsen

● Yokohama Royal Park Hotel   `Yokohama`

- 2-2-1-3 Minato-Mirai, Nishi-ku, Yokohama-shi, Kanagawa   • **TEL** (+81) 45-221-1111
- 603 rooms • http://www.yrph.com • VISA / MASTER / JCB / AMEX / DINERS
- Indoor pool, fitness facility, nursery room

● InterContinental Yokohama Grand   `Yokohama`

- 1-1-1 Minato-Mirai, Nishi-ku, Yokohama-shi, Kanagawa   • **TEL** (+81) 45-223-2323
- 594 rooms • http://www.ichotelsgroup.com • VISA / MASTER / JCB / AMEX / DINERS • Indoor pool, fitness facility, nursery room

● Pan Pacific Yokohama Bay Hotel Tokyu   `Yokohama`

- 2-3-7 Minato-Mirai, Nishi-ku Yokohama-shi, Kanagawa   • **TEL** (+81) 45-682-2222
- 480 rooms • http://pphy.co.jp • VISA / MASTER / JCB / AMEX / DINERS • Indoor pool, fitness facility, nursery room

● Rose Hotel Yokohama   `Yokohama`

- 77 Yamashitacho, Naka-ku, Yokohama-shi, Kanagawa   • **TEL** (+81) 45-681-3311
- 180 rooms • http://www.rosehotelyokohama.com • VISA / MASTER / JCB / AMEX / DINERS • Indoor pool, access to Yokohama Chinatown

● Fujiya Hotel   `Hakone/Kanagawa`

- 359 Miyanoshita, Hakone-machi, Ashigarashimo-gun, Kanagawa   • **TEL** (+81) 460-82-2211 • 146 rooms • http://www.fujiyahotel.jp • VISA / MASTER / AMEX / DINERS • Japanese-style inn, onsen, outdoor and indoor pool, spa

● Hotel de Yama   `Hakone/Kanagawa`

- 80 Motohakone, Hakone-machi, Ashigarashimo-gun, Kanagawa   • **TEL** (+81) 460-83-6321 • 89 rooms • http://www.odakyu-hotel.co.jp • VISA / MASTER / AMEX / DINERS / JCB • Onsen, open-air bath, spa, free pick-up service, free wi-fi, room with view of Mt. Fuji

○ Kansuiro `Yugawara/Kanagawa`

• 1300-20 Gora, Hakone-machi, Ashigarashimo-gun, Kanagawa • **TEL** (+81) 460-82-3141 • 14 rooms • http://www.kansuiro.co.jp • VISA / AMEX / DINERS / JCB
• Onsen, open-air bath

○ Ryotei Hanayura `Noboribetsu Onsen/Hokkaido`

• 100 Noboribetsu Onsen-cho, Noboribetsu-shi, Hokkaido • **TEL** (+81) 143-84-2322
• 37 rooms • http://www.hanayura.com • VISA / MASTER / JCB / AMEX / DINERS
• Japanese-style inn, onsen, room with open-air bath

○ Crawford Inn Onuma `Onuma/Hokkaido`

• 85-9 Onuma, Nanae-cho, Kameda-gun, Hokkaido • **TEL** (+81) 138-67-2964 • 30 rooms • http://crawford.jp • VISA / MASTER / JCB / AMEX / DINERS • Open-air bath, PC space

○ Grand Park Otaru `Otaru/Hokkaido`

• 11-3 Chikko, Otaru-shi, Hokkaido • **TEL** (+81) 134-21-3111 • 296 rooms • http://www.parkhotelgroup.com • VISA / MASTER / JCB / AMEX / DINERS / UNION PAY
• Access to golf course and ski resorts

○ Cross Hotel Sapporo `Sapporo/Hokkaido`

• 2-23 Kita-nijyo Nishi, Chuo-ku, Sapporo-shi, Hokkaido • **TEL** (+81) 11-272-0010
• 181 rooms • http://www.crosshotel.com • VISA / MASTER / JCB / AMEX / DINERS / UNION PAY • Open-air bath

○ JR Tower Hotel Nikko Sapporo `Hokkaido/Sapporo`

• 2-5 Kita-gojo Nishi, Chuo-ku, Sapporo-shi, Hokkaido • **TEL** (+81) 11-251-2222
• 350 rooms • http://www.jrhotels.co.jp • VISA / JCB / AMEX / DINERS • Spa, restaurant & bar

○ Loirsir Hotel Hakodate `Hokkaido/Hakodate`

• Nakadachiuri Shinmachi-dori, Kamigyo-ku, Kyoto-shi, Kyoto • **TEL** (+81) 75-441-4411 • 182 rooms • http://www.brightonhotels.co.jp • VISA / MASTER / JCB / AMEX / DINERS / UNION PAY • Outdoor pool, free pick up service

● La Vista Hakodate Bay   Hakodate/Hokkaido

- 12-6 Toyokawa-cho, Hakodate-shi, Hokkaido   • TEL (+81) 138-23-6111   • 356 rooms
- http://www.hotelspa.net/hotels/lahokodate   • VISA / MASTER / JCB / AMEX / DINERS   • Onsen, open-air bath

● Furano Hotel   Furano/Hokkaido

- Gakuden Sanku, Furano-shi, Hokkaido   • TEL (+81) 167-23-8111   • 25 rooms
- http://www.jyozankei-daiichi.co.jp   • VISA / MASTER / JCB / AMEX / DINERS
- Onsen, open-air bath, esthetic salon, free pick up service

● Best Western Hotel Newcity Hirosaki   Aomori

- 1-1-2 Omachi, Hirosaki-shi, Aomori   • TEL (+81) 172-37-0700   • 134 rooms   • TEL (+81) 172-37-0700   • http://www.bestwestern.co.jp   • VISA / MASTER / JCB / AMEX / DINERS   • PC space, Access to shopping mall

● Akita Castle Hotel   Akita

- 1-3-5 Naka-dori, Akita-shi, Akita   • TEL (+81) 18-834-1141   • 178 rooms   • http://www.castle-hotel.jp   • VISA / MASTER / JCB / AMEX / DINERS   • Access to clinics, spa, nail salon, convenience store

● Yamado   Iwate (Yukawa Onsen)

- 52-71-10 Yukawa, Nishi-Wagamachi, Waga-gun, Iwate   • TEL (+81) 197-82-2222
- 12 rooms   • http://www.yamado.co.jp   • VISA / MASTER / JCB / AMEX / DINERS
- Japanese-style inn, onsen, open-air bath, bangalows

● Chikusenso: Mt. Zao Onsen Resort & Spa   Miyagi (Togatta Onsen)

- 88-11 Aza Uwanohara, Togatta-onsen, Zao-machi, Katta-gun, Miyagi   • TEL (+81) 224-34-1188   • 30 rooms   • http://www.mtzaoresort.com   • VISA / MASTER / JCB / AMEX / DINERS   • Onsen, room with open-air bath

● Tokine-no-yado Yunushi Ichijoh   Miyagi (Togatta Onsen)

- 1-48 Azakamasaki, Fukuokakuramoto, Siraishi-shi, Miyagi   • TEL (+81) 224-26-2151
- 8 rooms   • http://www.ichijoh.co.jp   • VISA / MASTER / JCB / AMEX / DINERS
- Japanese-style inn, onsen, room with open-air bath

● Hotel Monterey Sendai `Miyagi`

- 4-1-8 Chuo, Aoba-ku, Sendai-shi, Miyagi ● **TEL** (+81) 22-265-7110 ● 206 rooms
- http://www.hotelmonterey.co.jp ● VISA / MASTER / JCB / AMEX / DINERS ● Free wi-fi, air-cleaner

● Meigetsuso `Yamagata (Kaminoyama Onsen)`

- 5-50 Hayama, Kaminoyama-shi, Yamagata ● **TEL** (+81) 23-672-0330 ● 20 rooms
- http://www.meigetsuso.co.jp ● VISA / MASTER / JCB / AMEX / DINERS ● Japanese-style inn, onsen, room with open-air bath

● Ginzan Onsen Fujiya `Yamgata/Tohoku`

- 443 Shinpata Oaza Ginzan, Obanazawa-shi, Yamagata ● **TEL** (+81) 237-28-2141
- 8 rooms ● http://www.fujiya-ginzan.com ● VISA / MASTER / DINERS ● Japanese-style inn, onsen

● Mercure Nagoya Cypress `Nagoya`

- 2-43-6 Meieki, Nakamura-ku, Nagoya-shi, Aichi ● **TEL** (+81) 52-571-0111 ● 115 rooms ● http://www.sofitelthecypress.com ● VISA / MASTER / JCB / AMEX / DINERS
- Access to Nagoya station

● Hilton Nagoya `Nagoya`

- 1-3-3 Sakae, Naka-ku, Nagoya-shi, Aichi ● **TEL** (+81) 52-212-1111 ● http://hilton-japan.ehotel-reserve.com ● VISA / MASTER / JCB / AMEX / DINERS ● Indoor pool, fitness facility

● Sakae no yu `Nagano (Asama Onsen)`

- 3-4-12 Asama-onsen, Matsumoto-shi, Nagano ● **TEL** (+81) 263-46-1031 ● 14 rooms ● http://www.sakaenoyu.com ● Japanese-style inn, onsen

● Otsuki Hotel Wafukan `Shizuoka`

- 3-9 Higashi-Kaigancho, Atami-shi, Shizuoka ● **TEL** (+81) 570-048-940 ● 24 rooms
- http://www.wafuukan.com ● Credit card : not available ● Japanese-style inn, rooms with open-air bath

● Shikinosato Kikuya | Niigata (Takanosu Onsen) |

- 1076-1 Takanosu, Sekikawa-mura, Iwafune-gun, Niigata • **TEL** (+81) 254-64-2393
- 9 rooms • http://www.takanosu.jp • Japanese-style inn, onsen, Open-air batsh, room with open-air bath, free pick up service

● Metropolitan Nagano Hotel | Nagano |

- 1346 Minami-Ishidocho, Nagano-shi, Nagano • **TEL** (+81) 26-291-7000 • 235 rooms • http://www.jrhotelgroup.com • VISA / MASTER / JCB / AMEX / DINERS
- Access to JR Nagano station

● Kinjohro | Ishikawa |

- 2-23 Hashibacho, Kanazawa-shi, Ishikawa • **TEL** (+81) 76-221-8188 • 3 rooms
- http://www.kinjohro.co.jp • VISA / MASTER / JCB / AMEX / DINERS • Ryotei (Japanese luxurious restaurant) style inn, onsen, Japanese garden

● Hotel Kanra Kyoto | Kyoto |

- 185 Karasumadori Rokujo Kudaru Kitamachi, Shimogyo-ku, Kyoto-shi, Kyoto • **TEL** (+81) 75-344-3815 • 7 rooms • http://www.hotelkanra.jp • VISA / MASTER / JCB / AMEX / DINERS • Onsen, Open-air bath, room with open-air bath, free pick up service

● Kyoto Brighton Hotel | Kyoto |

- Nakadachiuri Shinmachi-dori, Kamigyo-ku, Kyoto-shi, Kyoto • **TEL** (+81) 75-441-4411 • 182 rooms • http://www.brightonhotels.oo.jp • VISA / MASTER / JCB / AMEX / DINERS / UNION PAY • Outdoor pool, free pick up service

● The Screen | Kyoto |

- 640-1 Shimogoryomae-cho, Nakagyo-ku, Kyoto-shi, Kyoto • **TEL** (+81) 75-252-1113
- 13 rooms • http://www.screen-hotel.jp • VISA / MASTER / JCB / AMEX / DINERS
- Spa, access to Kyoto Imperial Palace

● Kizashi The Suite | Kyoto |

- 275 kitagawa, Gion-machi, Higashiyama-ku, Kyoto-shi, Kyoto • **TEL** (+81) 75-551-9600 • 8 rooms • http://www.kizashi-gion.jp • VISA / MASTER / JCB / AMEX / DINERS / UNION PAY • In-room spa, access to Gion

● Yuzuya Ryokan [Kyoto]

- 545 Minamitonari Yasaka-jinja, Minamigawa, Gion-machi, Higashiyama-ku, Kyoto-shi, Kyoto • **TEL** (+81) 75-533-6369 • 8 rooms • http://www.yuzuyaryokan.com • VISA / MASTER / JCB / AMEX / DINERS • Japanese-style inn, access to Gion

● Tawaraya [Kyoto]

- Anekoji Agaru, Fuyacho, Nakagyo-ku, Kyoto-shi, Kyoto • **TEL** (+81) 75-211-5566 • VISA / MASTER / JCB / AMEX / DINERS • 18 rooms • Japanese-style inn

● The Ritz-Carlton, Osaka [Osaka]

- 2-5-25 Umeda, Kita-ku, Osaka-shi, Osaka • **TEL** (+81) 6-6343-7000 • 292 rooms • http://www.ritzcarlton.com • VISA / MASTER / JCB / AMEX / DINERS • Indoor pool, fitness facility

● Hotel Hankyu International [Osaka]

- 19-19 Chayamachi, Kita-ku, Osaka-shi, Osaka • **TEL** (+81) 6-6377-2100 • 168 rooms • http://www.hankyu-hotel.com • VISA / MASTER / JCB / AMEX / DINERS • Spa, access to the station

● Hilton Osaka [Osaka]

- 1-8-8, Umeda, Kita-ku, Osaka-shi, Osaka • **TEL** (+81) 6-6347-7111 • 525 rooms • http://www1.hilton.com • VISA / MASTER / JCB / AMEX / DINERS • Indoor pool, fitness facility

● The Westin Osaka [Osaka]

- 1-1-20 Oyodonaka, Kita-ku, Oasaka-shi, Osaka • **TEL** (+81) 6-6440-1111 • 304 rooms • http://www.westin-osaka.co.jp • VISA / MASTER / JCB / AMEX / DINERS / UNION PAY • Indoor pool, fitness facility, nursery room, free pick up service

● Rihga Royal Hotel [Osaka]

- 5-3-68 Nakanoshima, Kita-ku, Osaka-shi, Osaka • **TEL** (+81) 6-6448-1121 • 974 rooms • http://www.rihga.com • VISA / MASTER / JCB / AMEX / DINERS / UNION PAY • Indoor pool, fitness facility, nursery room, free pick up service

⊙ Hotel Okura Kobe `Kobe`

• 2-1 Hatoba-cho, Chuo-ku, Kobe-shi, Hyogo • **TEL** (+81) 78-333-0111 • 475 rooms
• http://www.kobe.hotelokura.co.jp • VISA / MASTER / JCB / AMEX / DINERS / UNION
PAY • Indoor pool, Outdoor pool, fitness facility, nursery room, free pick up service

⊙ Hotel La Suite Kobe Harborland `Kobe`

• 7-2 Hatoba-cho, Chuo-ku, Kobe-shi, Hyogo • **TEL** (+81) 78-371-1111 • 70 rooms
• http://www.l-s.jp • VISA / MASTER / JCB / AMEX / DINERS / UNION PAY • Room
with ocean view, various spa facilities

⊙ Taketoritei Maruyama `Arima Onsen`

• 1364-1 Arima-cho, Kita-ku, Kobe-shi, Hyogo • **TEL** (+81) 78-904-0631 • 31 rooms
• http://www.taketoritei.com • VISA / MASTER / JCB / AMEX / DINERS / UNION PAY
• Onsen, private open-air bath (upon reservation)

⊙ Hotel Nikko Nara `Nara`

• 8-1 Sanjo-Hommachi, Nara-shi, Nara • **TEL** (+81) 742-35-8831 • 330 rooms
• http://www.jalhotels.com • VISA / MASTER / JCB / AMEX / DINERS / UNION PAY
• Spa, direct access to JR Nara station

⊙ Nara Hotel `Nara`

• 1096 Takahatacho, Nara-shi, Nara • **TEL** (+81) 742-26-3300 • 129 rooms • http://
www.narahotel.co.jp • VISA / MASTER / JCB / AMEX / DINERS • Japanese-style
rooms available, access to Nara park

⊙ Sheraton Hiroshima Hotel `Hiroshima`

• 12-1 Wakakusacho, Higashi-ku, Hiroshima-shi, Hiroshima • **TEL** (+81) 82-262-7111
• 238 rooms • http://www.sheraton-hiroshima.co.jp • VISA / MASTER / JCB / AMEX
/ DINERS / UNION PAY • Indoor pool, fitness facility • direct access to JR Hiroshima
station

⊙ Hotel Granvia Okayama `Okayama`

• 1-5 Ekimotomachi, Kita-ku, Okayama-shi, Okayama • **TEL** (+81) 86-234-7000
• 328 rooms • http://www.granvia-oka.co.jp • VISA / JCB / AMEX / DINERS • Indoor
pool, fitness facility • direct access to JR Okayama station

● Angkasa Hotel & Oriental Villa [Ehime]

• 129-5, Shimoidai-cho, Matsuyama-shi, Ehime • **TEL** (+81) 89-977-0003 • 31 rooms • http://www.angkasa.co.jp • VISA / MASTER / JCB / AMEX / DINERS • Room with open-air bath, various spa facilities

● Chiiori [Tokushima/Shikoku]

• 209 Tsurui, Higashi Iya, Miyoshi-shi, Tokushima • **TEL** (+81) 883-88-5290 • http://www.chiiori.org/ • Old village house • Weekend stay only (upon reservation), children under 6 years old not allowed. For reservation details check the web site

● Kotohira Kadan [Kagawa]

• 1241-5 Kotohira-cho, Nakatado-gun, Kagawa • **TEL** (+81) 877-75-3232 • 45 rooms • http://www.kotohira-kadan.jp • VISA / MASTER / JCB / AMEX / DINERS • Onsen, open-air bath, room with open-air bath, free pick up service

● Auberge Tosayama [Kochi]

• 661 Tosayama-Higashikawa, Kochi-shi, Kochi • **TEL** (+81) 88-850-6911 • 16 rooms • http://www.orienthotel.jp • VISA / MASTER / JCB / AMEX / DINERS • Restaurant-Inn, onsen, open-air bath, free pick up service

● With The Style Fukuoka [Fukuoka]

• 1-9-18 Hakataeki-minami, Hakata-Ku, Fukuoka-shi, Fukuoka • **TEL** (+81) 92-433-3900 • 16 rooms • http://www.withthestyle.com • VISA / MASTER / JCB / AMEX / DINERS • direct access to JR Hakata station

● Hakata Excel Hotel Tokyu [Fukuoka]

• 4-6-7, Nakasu, Hakata-ku, Fukuoka-shi, Fukuoka • **TEL** (+81) 92-262-0109 • 308 rooms • http://www.tokyuhotels.co.jp • VISA / MASTER / JCB / AMEX / DINERS • free wi-fi, PC space

● Sankara Hotel & Spa Yakushima [Kagoshima]

• 553 Haginoue, Mugio, Yakushima-cho, Kumage-gun, Kagoshima • **TEL** (+81) 997-47-3488 • 29 rooms • http://www.sankarahotel-spa.com • VISA / MASTER / JCB / AMEX / DINERS / UNION PAY • Outdoor pool, fitness facility, free pick up service

⦿ Hotel Nikko Huis Ten Bosch   Nagasaki

• 6 Huis Ten Bosch, Sasebo-shi, Nagasaki • **TEL** (+81) 956-27-3000 • 388 rooms
• http://www.nikko-htb.co.jp.com • VISA / JCB / AMEX • various spa facilities, access to Huis Ten Bosch

⦿ Kai Aso   Oita

• 628-6 Yutsubosenomoto, Kokonoe-cho, Kusu-gun, Oita • **TEL** (+81) 967-44-1000
• 12 rooms • http://www.kairesort.jp • VISA / MASTER / JCB / AMEX / DINERS • Onsen, open-air bath, room with open-air bath, free pick up service

⦿ Okinawa Kariyushi Urban Resort Naha   Okinawa

• 3-25-1, Maejima Naha-shi, Okinawa, Okinawa • **TEL** (+81) 98-860-2111 • 269 rooms • http://www.kariyushi.co.jp • VISA / MASTER / JCB / AMEX / DINERS / UNION PAY • Fitness facility, spa, free shuttle bus to/from the beach

⦿ Kohama Resort & Spa Nirakanai   Kohama Island

• 2954 Kohama, Taketomi-cho, Yaeyama-gun, Okinawa • **TEL** (+81) 980-84-6300
• 60 rooms • http://www.nanseirakuen.com • VISA / MASTER / JCB / AMEX / DINERS • Outdoor pool, free pick up service • Villa style rooms

⦿ Shigira Bayside Suite Allamana   Miyako Island

• 926-25 Ueno Shinzato, Miyakojima-shi, Okinawa • **TEL** (+81) 980-74-7100 • 174 rooms • http://www.nanseirakuen.com • VISA / MASTER / JCB / AMEX / DINERS • Free pick up service, next to Shigira Bay country club

⦿ Iriomote Sanctuary Resort Nirakanai   Iriomote Island

• 2-2 Uehara, Taketomi-cho, Yaeyama-gun, Okinawa • **TEL** (+81) 980-85-7111
• 140 rooms • http://www.nanseirakuen.com • VISA / JCB / AMEX / DINERS • Outdoor pool, free pick up service

⦿ The Terrace Club Wellness Resort At Busena   Okinawa

• 1750 Kise, Nago-shi, Okinawa • **TEL** (+81) 980-51-1111 • 68 rooms • http://www.terrace.co.jp • VISA / MASTER / JCB / AMEX / DINERS • Outdoor pool, fitness facility, various spa facilities

Tohoku Earthquake: How you can help

The Great East Japan Earthquake, together with the subsequent tsunami and the nuclear power plant disaster, has destroyed people's lives in Tohoku. Even today, hundreds of thousands of people are still being evacuated and much of the rubble along the coast line remains. The complete recovery will take years of aid work at many different levels. We can help remove the rubble. We can send food and aid materials. We can donate items or money. Here are some tremendous organizations that have been working really hard to support the people in the affected regions. Any small action counts!

Second Harvest Second Harvest collects and sends trucks of food and aid materials to evacuation centers in Tohoku. They need volunteers to collect, sort and load donation items as well as drivers. Please contact them for further information at the email address below.
Contact: volunteer@2hj.org
http://www.2hj.org/index.php/get_involved/donate_time (for volunteering)
http://www.2hj.org/index.php/eng_home (for general information about the organization)
Second Harvest is accepting donations. Please check their website below for further information.
http://www.2hj.org/index.php/get_involved/donate_money (for donations)

Peace Boat Peace Boat sends out volunteers to help with relief efforts in Ishinomaki City as well as to help raise donations in Tokyo. They offer an orientation seminar before sending out volunteers. Please contact Mr. Arata Otake at the email address below with your personal information (full name, age, gender, address, telephone number, email address, availability and language ability) as well as which location you are interested in volunteering.
Contact: arataotake@peaceboat.gr.jp
http://www.peaceboat.org/english/ (for general information about the organization)
Peace Boat is accepting donations. Secure online donations from overseas can be made via their affiliate Peace Boat US, using credit card or PayPal. (Peace Boat US is a registered 501(c) (3) nonprofit. organization)
http://www.peaceboat-us.org/

JEN (Japan Emergency NGOs) JEN dispatches various volunteer teams to support the victims of the Tohoku Earthquake. For further information, please check out their website below.

http://www.jen-npo.org/en

JEN is accepting donations to support a local NGO assisting the people of Tohoku. You can donate via their English online donation page below (donations accepted in Japanese Yen only).

http://www.jen-npo.org/en/involved/donate1.php

Tokyo English Life Line Tokyo English Life Line (TELL) provides free anonymous telephone counseling in English as well as offering professional face-to-face counseling and outreach programs . Please find more information on how to volunteer for TELL at their website below.

http://www.telljp.com/index.php?/en/volunteer

TELL is accepting donations to help run the organization. Please find more information at their website.

http://www.telljp.com/index.php?/en/how_to_donate

Association for Aid and Relief, Japan Association for Aid and Relief, Japan (AAR JAPAN) is an NGO that has been providing emergency assistance to people around the world since 1979. They have worked on a number of projects for the people of Tohoku, and are accepting donations to continue on their work. Please refer to the following website for details:

http://www.aarjapan.gr.jp/english (for general information)

http://www.aarjapan.gr.jp/english/ican/index.html (for donation)

Association of Medical Doctors of Asia (AMDA)

The Association of Medical Doctors of Asia is a non-governmental nonprofit organization founded in Okayama prefecture in 1984. They have been providing emergency medical aid to people affected by natural as well as man-made disasters around the world, and are continuing to provide medical aid in the Tohoku area. You can help their work by making a donation. Please check the following website for more details:

http://www.amdainternational.com/english (about donations)

http://www.amdainternational.com/english/about/index.html (about AMDA)

Foreign Volunteers Japan Foreign Volunteers Japan provides an open forum to share and discuss information regarding volunteer activities, aid delivery and humanitarian relief issues concerning the post-tsunami recovery of the Tohoku region. For the latest information on volunteering to help people in Tohoku, please check out their website.

(website information goes here: http://foreignvolunteersjapan.blogspot.com/)

A to Z INDEX

Photo courtesies and many thanks to:

Alan (A) Seki
Chiiori Trust
Hiroki Nishioka
Jared Braiterman
Jishu-jinja Shrine
JNTO
Kansuiro Ryokan
Nakano Broadway Shoten-gai Shinko Kumiai
Nakatsugawa City
Sapporo Lion Inc.
Shirakawa Village
TCVB (Tokyo Convention & Visitors Bureau)
Yamaroku Shoyu

Cover design: Masayoshi Nakajo

With over 50 years of experience, Nakajo is one of Japan's notable graphic designers. His works include Shiseido, Matsuya Ginza, the Museum of Contemporary Art Tokyo, and the official logo of Chiba prefecture. He is also known as the art director for *Hanatsubaki*, Shiseido's style magazine. His design is favored by many generations, and he has received Tokyo ADC golden awards several times.

"Japan Visions" photography: Kishin Shinoyama

Shinoyama graduated from Nihon University and worked with the Light Publicity agency while he was still a student. After leaving Light Publicity in 1968 to work as a freelancer, he began a successful career photographing subjects which ranging from portraits of pop stars to documenting the Great Earthquake, capturing scenes with a fine expressive technique. His unique character and appearance made him a media star. He has already launched over 300 titles including *Balthus: The Painter's House*.

Editorial Director: Masanobu Sugatsuke

Sugatsuke has been involved with cultural and fashion editorial projects for more than 25 years, producing a number of timely and epochal works. He has managed and edited magazines such as *Composite, Invitation, Ecocolo, Libertines* as well as books featuring Elizabeth Peyton, Mark Borthwick, Jeff Burton, Daido Moriyama, and Kishin Shinoyama. He is the author of *The Edit of Tokyo* and *Editorial Paradise,* and was awarded a NY ADC Silver Prize.

Editing and planning: WAttention

WAttention Co., Ltd. is a publisher of *WAttention*, a free English magazine focusing on introducing tourism, culture, heritage, arts as well as the latest trends of Japan. The magazine been distributed at more than 500 places in the Asian tourism hub Singapore, including airports, major hotels and restaurants. WAttention also publishes *Wattention Tokyo* and partners with regional publishers to provide contents to other regions, such as *WAttention* Malaysia and soon to launch US edition.

Editorial director: Masanobu Sugatsuke for Sugatsuke Office., Ltd.
Editorial staff: Yaeko Inaba, Mizuho Ota, Taeko Takeyama, Kiyomi Fujioka
Editorial assistances: Katia Wong, Ayano Shiraishi, Ayumi Itokawa
Minook International(S)Pte Ltd.
Cover design: Masayoshi Nakajo
"Japan Visions" photography: Kishin Shinoyama
Interior page design: Yasuhisa Tamura

TRAVEL GUIDE TO AID JAPAN

2011年8月25日　第1刷発行

編者：Masanobu Sugatsuke & WAttention Co., Ltd.
発行人：鈴木康子

発行所：和テンション株式会社
〒107-0062 東京都港区南青山5-18-10-202
TEL：03-6418-5701　FAX：03-6862-6760
WEB：www.wattention.com

印刷/製本：凸版印刷株式会社 Toppan Printing Co., Ltd.

© WAttention Co., Ltd. 2011 Printed in Japan
ISBN 978-4-905488-00-2